EASY BEER MAKING
REAL ALE IN 21 DAYS

MARK KAYE

Easy Beer Making

◆

Real Ale in 21 days

HAMLYN
LONDON · NEW YORK · SYDNEY · TORONTO

First published in 1984 by
The Hamlyn Publishing Group Limited
London · New York · Sydney · Toronto
Astronaut House, Feltham, Middlesex, England

© Copyright
The Hamlyn Publishing Group Limited 1984

Illustrated by Ann Rees

Cover photography by James Jackson

ISBN 0 600 30552 X

Printed in Yugoslavia

Contents

Introduction

Mankind has been brewing an alcoholic beverage from cereals for some 5000 years or more. It follows that, with all our modern technology, making beer at home today must be easy. For centuries brewing was exclusively the domain of women. As recently as 1599 Mistress Quickly, in Shakespeare's play *The Merry Wives of Windsor*, Act 1, Scene 4, refers to her ability to "brew and bake", and indeed many women today brew excellent beer for their families. However, brewing their own beer has also become the hobby of many men and not only those who have retired.

Compared with no more than a century ago, brewing at home has become incredibly easy. It now takes only minutes rather than hours to start a brew; fermentation looks after itself; and, with plastic kegs readily available, draught beer can be put away in minutes. Within a few days to a week or more you can have the first glass of your brew in your hand, although it won't stay there long! What's more, you can make bitter beer, light ale, lager, brown ale, stout and, with a little more patience, barley wine, the king of beers. You can make your favourite beer, too, in the quantities you require, from 16 to 40 pints at a time.

The very minimum of equipment is needed: a polythene bin in which to brew the beer, a plastic paddle with which to stir it, and a polythene tube with which to siphon it into the keg or into bottles. If bottles are used, crown caps and a crimping tool will be required.

The criticism of so many beers today is that they are often weak, often thin and often gassy. At home you can brew as strong a beer as you want with as much body as you want and, by natural ferment, with only as much gas as you want. There is no doubt, then, that home-brewed beer is real ale and it is quick and easy to make.

But there is more to beer than brewing it. Some of the pleasure of drinking beer comes from the environment or atmosphere of the place where you are drinking it and the company with whom you are drinking. Many people enjoy having a glass or two of their favourite beer with their friends in their local pub. It is somewhere to go to escape from the pressures of work and the chores of home, somewhere to meet convivial, like-minded company, where you can have a game of darts, chance your arm on a 'bandit', listen to the piano and join in a song. It is in fact a place where you can relax and be yourself.

All this is true and has made the British pub a place that Britons have taken abroad wherever they have gone. Most Continental holiday centres catering for British people boast of a pub as one of their attractions. It is a great institution that, in one form or another, has been around for a very long time. We know that the Egyptians had ale houses some 4000 years ago. We know that England had so many ale houses in the 10th century that King Edgar allowed each village to have only one and closed all the others. So what is the point of brewing your own beer if you are going to miss your pub?

Brewing beer brings another and a different kind of satisfaction. There is not only the pleasure of drinking a really good ale but the satisfaction of having made it yourself, with a texture and a taste to suit your own palate. There is, too, the pleasure of having the beer readily available, just when you fancy it. If you have been gardening, decorating or cleaning the car and feel like a beer at that very moment, the beer is ready and waiting. You don't have to clean up, walk a distance, or even drive a distance, your favourite beer is there to be had. No matter how foul the weather, the pouring rain or biting wind that keeps you at home doesn't keep you from your favourite beer. But there's more to it than that. There is the fellowship of other home brewers. Fishermen's tales? Gardeners' talk? Don't forget the brewers' yarns! There is much pleasure in sharing a beer with another home brewer: an opportunity to evaluate the colour and clarity, the firm head and lively bead, the aroma of malt and hops, the clean taste and the flavoursome tang, and to enjoy the feeling of satisfaction that pervades one's whole being. It is an occasion for discussing the ingredients and method, the manufacture of a kit beer, the choice of ingredients, including malt grains, malt syrup, or malt flour, adjuncts, the hop variety, and the very

water itself that plays such an important part in the brewing of a good beer. Grain mashing and sparging provide endless conversation, for all the variations are reflected in the finished brew. The pleasures of drinking your own beer are quite different and much more rewarding.

But there is more to home brew than even all this. Quality and availability are important but so, too, is cost. Depending on the price of beer in your local, you can brew as good as you can buy and often better, for about one tenth the price. There is no excise duty or V.A.T., there are no overheads, distribution and labour costs on home-brewed beer, so you must be on to a winner.

The ingredients cost money, of course, but the savings are so great that it is always worth buying the best. Your outlay on equipment will be a few pounds, but this can be used so often that the cost per pint can be ignored. It also takes a little time and trouble to brew the beer, but so does a pot of tea! After a few times a routine is developed and the various processes can be carried out without reference to books or recipes. Making beer becomes as automatic as making a pot of tea.

Styles you can brew

The number of different beers that you can brew is beyond count. Every small variation in the quality or quantity of an ingredient, in the mix of the ingredients, and in the method of brewing will result in a slightly different beer. Nevertheless, there are certain general styles into which most beers fit.

Bitter

The most popular kind of beer in the United Kingdom is undoubtedly draught bitter, and this can be made in two ways, casked and bottled. In the home it is probably true that more beer is bottled than casked. Although the same wort may be fermented, for both bottle and cask, the resulting beers will have a different taste. All bitter-style beers should be brewed with hard water.

Draught bitter should be clear and free from haze but is rarely as bright as the bottled version. Similarly, whilst draught bitter should pour with a good head and condition, a bottled beer should hold its head and condition a little longer.

There are four main divisions of the bitter-style beer. The first is what might be called "common" or "everyday" bitter. The second is sometimes described as "best bitter", or Burton bitter, or export ale. Both should have a good copper colour and a noticeable taste of malt and hops. The original gravity of the first should be around 1.040, and of the second around 1.046. Both these beers should taste dry and full-bodied, the second slightly more so than the first.

The third division is usually called pale ale and the fourth light ale. Light ale is by definition light in colour, body and alcohol. An original gravity between 1.030 and 1.034 is adequate for this bitter. The beer should be straw-coloured and brilliantly clear, very pleasing to the eye. The lower malt quantity should be matched by a lower hop content, so that a good balance of flavour is achieved. As its name implies the beer should be thirst-quenching without being intoxicating. It makes a good beer to drink at midday and is sometimes called a luncheon ale.

Pale ale comes between best bitter and light ale in colour, flavour, texture and strength. The original gravity should be between 1.036 and 1.040. Pale ale is nearly always bottled and makes an attractive aperitif for those who like a glass of beer before a meal. The slightly more pronounced malt and hop flavour has a tangy freshness that cleanses the palate.

Lager

This beer has become increasingly popular in recent years, probably as a result of holidays on the Continent. It has as many variations as bitter beers, ranging from the light, crisp, tangy and golden lagers to the full-bodied, smooth strong and amber Continental lagers. The original gravity can vary from 1.038 to 1.060! Soft water should always be used in the brewing of lagers and the wort should always be fermented with a Carlsbergensis yeast. The more delicately flavoured Haller-tau or Saaz hops should be used instead of British hops. The best results are obtained from a lager malt or malt extract and a long, slow fermentation under an airlock. Even so, it is not easy to make really good lagers in the home. Many of them turn out to be a splendid pale ale. But then, few British-made commercial lagers are comparable with Continental lagers.

Stout

Here again there are sub-divisions of the main style, although both must be brewed with soft water. Dry, or Irish stout as it is sometimes called, is the more popular. It is jet-black in colour and should have a closely grained head the colour of a dark oatmeal. The head should be significant and long-lasting. The beer should be full-bodied and have a clean, bitter taste, completely lacking in sweetness. The original gravity should lie between 1.044 and 1.046. For some reason stout is very popular with women. It also has the reputation of being beneficial to those recovering from an illness or an operation and is sometimes given to patients in hospitals, and convalescent homes.

Sweet or milk stout is the other half of this division. The taste should be more malty than hoppy, so the sugar and hops content should be kept low. The sweetening comes from the addition of lactose, the sugar found in milk: hence the reference to milk stout. No milk in any form is included in the ingredients. The black colour is not usually quite so deep as that in dry stout and may even contain a hint of brown. The head, too, may be a shade lighter in colour than that on the dry version. The original gravity should be in the region of 1.034 to 1.036. A variation of this formula includes oatmeal, which gives the beer yet another flavour.

Brown Ale

This is a style quite distinct from bitter and stout and not just a blend of the two. There are, indeed, numerous variations of brown ale, particularly between the north and the south of England. The colour ranges from a very dark amber to a brownish black. The Newcastle brown ales have a noticeable bitterness; the London brown ales are just as noticeably smooth. All brown ales should have a sweetish taste resulting from a high dextrin content achieved in the mashing process. The alcohol content is quite low, however, since the original gravity should be nearer to 1.030 than 1.034. Lactose may be used for sweetening if necessary.

Barley Wine

This is the last of the major styles. It is a very strong beer with an alcohol content of about 10%, equal to some table wines. For this reason it is usually matured in half-pint bottles and served in five-ounce goblets. The colour should be a deep copper brown. Whilst the beer should have a good bead of condition, the high alcohol content is not likely to support much of a head. The beer should be very full-bodied with a strong malty flavour. The texture should be very smooth. The high hop content and long boiling provide the tannin to preserve the beer for the long maturation necessary to harmonize the high malt and, therefore, high alcohol content. Hard water must be used and experience shows that a Champagne wine yeast produces a good barley wine under home conditions. Barley wine is an outstanding beverage when well made.

Other Beers

There is a range of beverages called beer that are not made from malt and hops and others that are based on malt and hops but contain unusual additional ingredients. Recipes for some of them are given later. Suffice here to mention the well-known ginger beer, honey beer and spruce beer. Ginger beer is made from a weak sugar solution flavoured with ginger; honey beer is made from a solution of honey flavoured with hops; and spruce beer is made from a malt solution flavoured with essences from the spruce fir tree.

Some strong beers can be flavoured with fruits like morello cherries or damsons, or even pieces of cooked chicken. They are great fun to make in one-gallon quantities for serving on special occasions to appreciative company. They are not suitable for everyday drinking.

13

Brewers' talk

Acetic Describes the sour taste of vinegar occasionally found in a beer that has been left exposed to the air and has been infected by acetic acid fungi.

Adjuncts Ingredients other than malt and hops used in brewing to vary the flavour and body or to increase the alcohol content of a beer. Flaked rice or flaked maize are examples.

Alcohol The spirit formed during fermentation which gives beer much of its enjoyable and satisfying taste.

Ale A word once used to describe a beverage fermented from a malt solution before hops were used for flavouring – an unhopped beer. It now means the same as beer.

Attenuation The reduction of the original gravity of a wort during fermentation; more precisely, the thinning of a malt and sugar solution.

Autolysis The decomposition of dead yeast cells and the use of the nitrogen thus released by the remaining live cells.

Balm or Barm A name once used to describe yeast.

Beer The name now given to all beverages fermented from a malt solution and flavoured with hops. Formerly applied only to hopped ales when some were not so flavoured.

Body The fullness or density of a beer often caused by the presence of unfermentable sugars, such as dextrins.

Bottled Beer A beer that undergoes a secondary fermentation in the bottle. It is usually brighter in colour than a draught beer. Commercial bottled beers are generally simply impregnated with carbon dioxide from a gas cylinder and do not undergo a secondary fermentation.

Bottles These are usually dark brown in colour, very strong, and able to withstand the pressure caused by the secondary fermentation. Only proper beer bottles should be used for home-brewed beer. Screw-stoppered spirit bottles and wine bottles should be avoided.

Brewer's Yeast A mixture of different strains of a globular-shaped yeast known as *saccharomyces cerevisiae*, and used exclusively in the fermentation of hop-flavoured malt solutions. It ferments very rapidly, mostly on the surface of the wort. Sometimes sold as 'beer yeast' or 'stout yeast', it is not to be confused with lager yeast (*see* entry).

Bru Keg A pressurized plastic container that was developed for use by home brewers. It is translucent, has graduated markings, a draw-off tap, a close-fitting screw cap and facilities for the provision of a CO_2 injector. There are a number of versions available.

Burton Water Hard water containing a number of mineral salts, particularly calcium sulphate and magnesium sulphate, especially beneficial in the mashing of grains for bitter beers. Any water can now be burtonized by the addition of hardening salts. Originally Burton water flowed copiously from the springs at Burton-on-Trent. So many breweries were situated there that Burton became known as the beer town of England.

Calcium Sulphate Otherwise known as gypsum, is a constituent of Burton water and packets of hardening salts.

Capping Tool An instrument devised for the home brewer to assist with the sealing of beer bottles by crimping on crown caps.

Caramel A substance made by heating sugar with ammonium salts and used for darkening beer. It should be used in moderation.

Carbohydrates All those starch- and sugar-containing ingredients used in the brewing of beer.

Carbon Dioxide The gas given off during fermentation. During the secondary fermentation it is retained in the beer and imparts liveliness and freshness. It is also available in small capsules for injecting into a keg of draught beer to impart liveliness.

CO_2 Injector A device that can be fitted to a plastic pressure keg so that a controlled quantity of carbon dioxide can be introduced into the beer.

Condition The liveliness of a mature beer. Poor condition is indicated by lack of rising bubbles, by flatness and by dullness. Beer in good condition has a good head supported by a steady stream of rising bubbles and has life and vitality.

Crown Caps Metal domes lined with cork or plastic that can be crimped on to a bottle to give it a gas-tight seal.

Dextrins Complex sugar molecules that can be fermented only slowly and sometimes remain in a beer, giving it body and a little sweetness. They are formed during the mashing of the malted barley grains. Their presence masks the quantity of fermentable sugar in a wort.

Diastase A mixture of alpha and beta amylase formed during the malting of the barley grain. It reduces the starch in the grain to maltose and dextrin during the mashing period. It is very sensitive to heat and the difference of one degree centigrade/two degrees Fahrenheit varies the quantity of maltose or dextrin produced.

D.M.S. An abbreviation for diastatic malt syrup. This is a toffee-like malt extract that contains some diastase enzymes, useful in reducing the starch of adjuncts to fermentable sugars.

Draught Beer A beer that undergoes a secondary fermentation or carbonation in a large container and is drawn off through a tap. The opposite of bottled beer.

Dry A beer that has no taste of sweetness.

Dry Hopping The addition of a handful or so of hop flowers or a few hop pellets, or even a few drops of hop oil, in the middle period of fermentation. A fresh, tangy hop flavour is imparted to the beer.

End Point The completion of the conversion of the starch in the malt grains and the adjuncts into maltose and dextrin during the mashing process. It is recognized by the failure of a tablespoonful of the wort to change colour after the addition of a drop or two of iodine.

Enzymes Protein molecules joined to an organic compound that act as catalysts, that is, substances which cause changes in the make-up and structure of other molecules without being themselves changed. Many enzymes are involved in the brewing of beer, each one responsible for a single different activity.

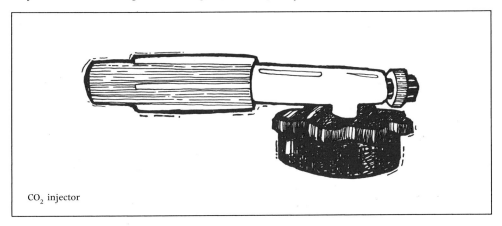

CO_2 injector

Fermentation The conversion of maltose and sucrose to alcohol and carbon dioxide by the different enzymes and co-enzymes contained in the apo-zymase group that are secreted by the *saccharomyces cerevisiae* yeast cells (brewer's yeast).

Fermentation Bin A natural polythene bin with a lid and carrying handle used for the fermentation of the wort into beer. Fermentation bins are of differing sizes: 10, 15 and 25 litres.

Finings Substances, usually gelatine or isinglass, that may be added to a hazy beer to clarify it. They should always be used in accordance with the manufacturer's instructions.

Flake The name given to an adjunct that has already been processed from a grain to a thin flake. The most popular adjuncts are flaked rice and flaked maize, but flaked wheat and flaked barley may also be used.

Flocculence A swirl of millions of yeast cells caused by a faulty yeast that occurs whenever a container is moved in which there is a finished beer to be racked. Most yeasts settle firmly on the bottom of a bin.

Fobbing Froth that gushes from a bottle of mature beer when the seal is removed. It can be brought on by over-priming or by storing and serving the beer at too high a temperature.

Fretting An occurrence in draught beer similar to fobbing in bottled beer.

Gallon A standard measure for beer up to 36 gallons, a quantity known as a barrel. A gallon consists of 8 pints, each of 20 fluid ounces, and is the equivalent of 4.54 litres. A U.S. gallon also consists of 8 pints but these are each made up of only 16 fluid ounces.

Glucose The name given to a single sugar derived from sucrose (household sugar) or maltose. It is sometimes added to a wort to increase the alcohol content. Glucose is available both in lumps, called chips, and as a powder.

Goods An alternative word for grist.

Grist The grain or mixture of grains used in the brewing of beer. The whole grains must first be crushed to release the starch from the bran, hence the phrase 'all grist to the mill'.

Head The collection of froth that forms on the surface of the beer when it is poured into a glass. It has an attractive appearance and increases the appeal of a beer. Sadly, it does not last long on some beers.

Heading Liquid or Powder A substance that can be added during the brewing of a beer to reduce the surface tension when it is poured. This slows down the rate at which the bubbles of carbon dioxide burst and so retains the froth for longer.

Hops The cone-shaped flowers from the hop bine, *humulus lupulus*, that are boiled with a malt solution to impart a bitter, tangy flavour. They also have preservative qualities. Hops are available as dried, loose flowers, as pressed flowers, as pellets from which much of the dross of petals and stalks has been removed, and as hop oil containing only the essential oils and resins of the hops. There are several different varieties of hops suitable for the different beers brewed.

Hot Break The separation of the proteins from the malt and hop solution during boiling.

Invert Sugar A simple mixture of fructose and glucose prepared by boiling sucrose (household sugar) with citric acid for 20 minutes. Invert sugar is immediately fermentable and therefore often used in brewing to facilitate a quick conversion to alcohol.

Irish Moss A seaweed, also known as carragheen moss, that is dried and powdered for use during the boiling stage of brewing. It helps to clarify the wort prior to fermentation.

Krausening The addition of unfermented wort instead of priming sugar to a beer about to be bottled or casked, usually at the rate of 5% of the whole. Thus, in a five-gallon brew (40 pints) two pints of unfermented wort would be reserved for priming the 38 pints of fermented wort.

Lactose An unfermentable sugar used for sweetening brown ales and stouts.

Lager Yeast Known as *saccharomyces Carlsbergensis*, it ferments more slowly than brewer's yeast, at a lower temperature and from the bottom of the wort. It can also ferment certain other sugars so that lager beer becomes quite dry.

Lees The deposit of dead yeast cells and other insoluble particles that settles on the bottom of containers after fermentation. The clearing beer should be removed from them to avoid the development of unpleasant flavours.

Liquor Water that has been adjusted for hardness or softness and is to be used for brewing. Beer is made from malt, hops and liquor.

Lupulin The golden-coloured powder found at the base of the hop petals. It contains the essential oils and resin for flavouring and preserving the beer.

Malt Barley grains that have been artificially sprouted and then kilned.

Maltase The enzyme that converts maltose into glucose.

Malt Extract A liquor in which malt grains have been mashed until the starch has been converted to maltose and then concentrated to a toffee-like constituency.

Malt Flour A malt extract that has been spun-dried to produce a flour.

Maltose The sugar produced from starch by the diastase enzymes.

Malt Syrup Another name for malt extract.

Mash The mixture of crushed malts, adjuncts and liquor.

Mashing The process of converting the starch in the mash to maltose by steeping it at a certain temperature for several hours.

Mashing Bin A container used for mashing grains. It can be obtained, suitably lagged, with a draw-off tap beneath a mesh supporting the grains and a variable thermostat.

Original Gravity The specific gravity of a malt prior to fermentation. Not all the wort is fermentable because of the presence of dextrin.

Pitch The addition of an activated yeast to a wort.

Pressure Keg A rigid plastic container with a draw-off tap and fitted with a tight-sealing screw cap. It is able to withstand the pressures of secondary fermentation and is ideal for draught beers. Pressure kegs are available in several sizes and types.

Priming The addition of a precise quantity of unfermented wort or sugar to a fermented wort, in order to cause a controlled secondary fermentation in the beer and thus give it liveliness and appeal.

Rack To remove a clear or clearing beer from its deposit of lees. This is usually done with the aid of a siphon.

Raw Grain Any grain used in the mash other than malted barley grains.

Ropiness An oily appearance in a beer caused by the presence of lactic acid bacteria that do not separate from each other and so form 'ropes'. Not very common, it can be cured and is easily prevented by good hygiene.

Rouse To stir up the wort, especially after skimming and during fermentation. The action removes carbon dioxide and introduces some air into the wort to enable the yeast to reproduce itself and maintain a vigorously fermenting colony.

Sparging The action of removing all traces of maltose from mashed grains by slowly spraying hot water over them.

Specific Gravity The weight of a given volume of a liquid compared with the same volume of water at a temperature of $15°C/59°F$ and measured by a hydrometer.

Starch The polysaccharide (complex sugar) found in cereals of all kinds. It forms the largest portion of the carbohydrates that are converted into alcohol during the process of brewing beer.

Sucrose Household sugar. It is mostly used in its white, granulated form to increase the carbohydrates in a wort, and can also be used for priming. Sucrose consists of a combination of the two single sugars, glucose and fructose.

Sulphite The popular name for sodium or potassium metabisulphite. When dissolved in water this white powder releases the gas, sulphur dioxide, which kills or inhibits the growth of bacteria. It is widely used for sterilizing otherwise clean containers of all kinds but especially bins and bottles.

Sweet A beer containing a significant quantity of residual dextrins and/or malto-dextrins or added lactose. The opposite of dry.

Thin Describes the watery texture caused by the absence of residual carbohydrates. The presence of too much alcohol can also cause thinning. The opposite of fullness and body.

Torrified Barley Unmalted barley grains that have been heated in such a way as to cause them to swell out like small popcorns. Sometimes used as an adjunct.

Wheat The cereal mostly used for making bread but which is sometimes used as an adjunct in the form of flakes (Weetabix), or in a brewing flour (Brumore), or in the form of a syrup.

Wort The name given to a solution of maltose, dextrins, sucrose, hop oils, resins and colouring, prior to fermentation into beer. The liquor strained from a mash is also called wort.

Yeast The single-cell fungi known as *saccharomyces cerevisiae* that secrete the enzymes capable of converting wort into beer. The yeast, *saccharomyces Carlsbergensis*, converts an appropriate wort into lager.

Zymase The complex of enzymes that reduce glucose to alcohol and carbon dioxide.

The things you need

Although you can get by with very little equipment, especially if you make only kit beer, it is worth buying some good equipment so that you can make other beers as well.

Whatever beer you brew you will need a polythene **fermentation bin**. Avoid coloured dustbins since they are sometimes made from recycled plastics and may, in addition, be coloured with a substance, such as cadmium, that could be injurious to health. Polythene fermentation bins are purpose-made for home-brewers from good-quality material. They are available in assorted sizes from 10 to 25 litres/$2\frac{1}{4}$ to $5\frac{1}{2}$ gallons. Always use one larger than the quantity of beer being brewed, since some space must be left for the froth. Furthermore, the pliable polythene constricts the volume of a full bin when lifted and moved to another place and could cause spillage. Fermentation bins have a fitting lid and a carrying handle. Most of them also have graduated markings on one side in litres and gallons and some have a draw-off tap at the bottom.

A long-handled **plastic paddle** will be needed for stirring. Plastic is safer than wood because it is easier to sterilize and is less likely to be used for other culinary purposes.

Fermentation bins and plastic paddle

A large stainless steel or aluminium **boiling pan** with a lid will be needed, even for kit brewing. For malt extract and hops or for grains and hops, a boiling pan is essential for boiling the hops in the wort.

A plastic **siphon** is needed when filling bottles. One with a J tube at one end and a small tap at the other works excellently in practice. The shape of the J tube causes the clear beer to be sucked down into the tube. Without the bend the beer would be sucked up off the sediment and could so disturb it that some sediment could be carried over into the bottles. The tap at the other end of the tube enables you to regulate the flow and avoid spillage between bottles.

Proper heavy-duty, returnable **beer bottles** are essential. Light-weight, non-returnable bottles are sometimes used by commercial breweries, especially for beer bought from supermarkets and similar outlets. However, it is dangerous for the home brewer to use them because it is very difficult to control precisely the pressure generated in the bottle. It is possible for such a bottle to burst when it is picked up and the pressure disturbed. Only strong, returnable beer bottles can therefore be recommended and it is worth buying them for their safety. They can be used hundreds of times, so that their cost per pint becomes infinitesimal. No other type of bottle should ever be employed.

Boiling pan, siphon and beer bottles

Depending on the method of closure of the bottles, you will need good-quality rubber washers for **screw stoppers**, or plastic-lined **crown caps** and a **crimping tool**. Plastic-lined caps are easier to sterilize than those that are lined with cork. Crimping instruments can be as simple as a hammer and a capping tool shaped like a little saucepan attached upside down to a wooden handle. On the other hand they may consist of a two-handed lever tool that holds the cap on a magnet until it is safely crimped, or a table model, beneath which the bottle is placed, the cap being crimped by a downward pull of a single lever.

Attractive **labels** naming the style of beer and the date it was brewed give a professional appearance to the finished bottle. Plastic crates are handy for moving and storing the maturing beer.

Enthusiastic brewers will want to use some grains and these need additional equipment. An electric **blender**, a coffee bean **grinder** or a **mincer** can be used for crushing the grains, although these can usually be bought already crushed.

A **mashing vessel** will be needed for the steeping process. The ideal is a large electric boiler fitted with a very sensitive and adjustable thermostat. It should have a draw-off tap and be fitted with a fine-meshed, stainless-steel false bottom on which the crushed grains can lie just above the tap. A close-fitting lid and a blanket for insulation complete the requirements.

There are alternatives, however, and a large, insulated food container, as used by campers, is an excellent substitute if it has a draw-off tap, or if you can fit one yourself. The container will maintain an even temperature in the mash without difficulty. Care must be taken to ensure that the inlet to the tap is adequately protected from being clogged up by the mash. One way to do this is to place the grains in a strong nylon bag (not a stocking or tights, for these may well split during the stirring in).

Another alternative is the fermentation bin well lagged with blankets. An **immersion heater** can also be used to heat the water to the required temperature. A long

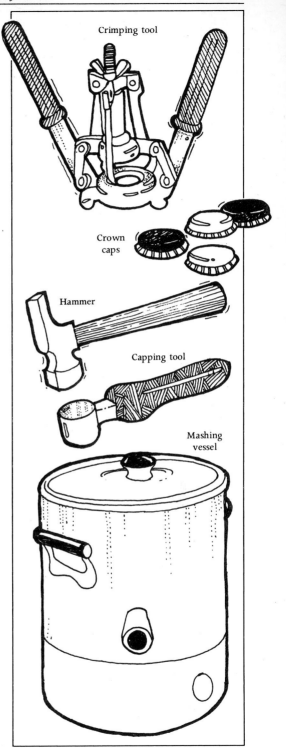

Crimping tool

Crown caps

Hammer

Capping tool

Mashing vessel

Items needed include (1) a calico bag and metal stand, (2) a thermometer, (3) polythene funnels, (4) a hydrometer and (5) a trial jar.

thermometer is obviously necessary, which is best kept in its case when not in use.

After the grains have been mashed the maltose has to be washed out of them. The mashing vessel need not be very large, for you can mash 1.35 kg/3 lb of grains in 4.5 litres/1 gallon of water, but a good supply of hot water will be required for the sparging. A strong **calico bag** fitted to a metal stand that can be placed over a collecting vessel has been designed for the home brewer, but it is often possible to adapt the facilities already available. The actual spraying of hot water over the grains can be carried out using a watering can rose or by moving a narrow tube about over the top of the grains.

A **hydrometer** and **trial jar** are needed for checking the original gravity of the wort and the finished gravity of the beer. In addition, an assortment of **polythene funnels** is always useful. A **record book** should also be kept of the beers brewed, the in-

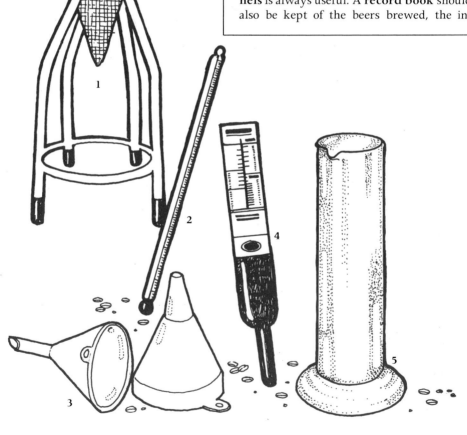

gredients used, the method followed, including length of mash, temperature, boiling times, etc.

For lovers of draught beers a fine assortment of **pressure kegs** are available in different sizes and with different fittings to maintain the pressure. For hygiene a **bottle brush** is desirable. Buy one with a handle long enough to scrub the inside of bins and kegs as well as bottles.

A visit to a specialist home brew centre is well worthwhile, for there you will see the widest range of different pieces of equipment. It is also a good idea to obtain the catalogues of several mail order firms. They advertise in the monthly magazine, 'The Amateur Winemaker and Home Brewer', which is published in South Street, Andover, Hants.

Take care of your equipment, keep it clean and stored in a dry place, and always sterilize each piece before use.

A further selection of essential or useful equipment: (1) labels, (2) record book, (3) bottle brushes and (4) pressure container (pressure keg).

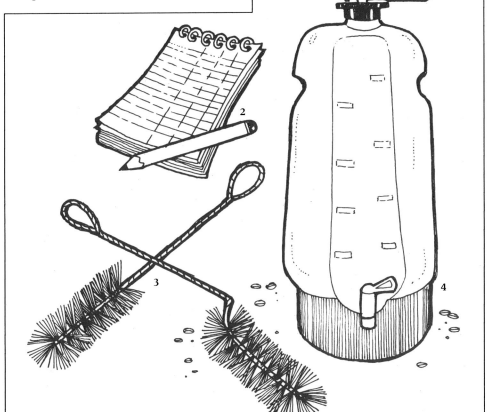

What goes into beer

Beer is brewed from malt, hops and liquor, with the occasional addition of adjuncts to vary the flavour and texture.

Malt

Although all cereals can be malted, barley is nowadays used almost exclusively for making beer. In a few places on the Continent a small quantity of wheat is malted in preparation for making so-called 'white beer'. In parts of Africa and the United States maize is the ingredient but in Great Britain wheat and maize are used only as adjuncts to the barley.

There are different varieties of barley as there are of most plants and brewers prefer those varieties with a lower nitrogen content. Having selected his grain, the maltster sifts out any foreign bodies and soaks the barley in water for some hours. This is to soften the grain and increase the moisture content so that the necessary enzymes can develop. He then lays the seeds out several inches deep on the warm floor of his maltings.

Once or twice a day he turns them over so that each grain gets an equal amount of warmth and begins to sprout at both ends – one producing tiny hairlike roots, the other the embryonic stem. The warmth and moisture that germinate the seed enable an enzyme called cytase to break down the tough, protective cellulose skin surrounding the starch that would be the food for the young plant until it could feed itself. The proteolytic enzymes then break down the protein between the starch cells, and the hard mass of starch is changed to a soft, friable texture.

The process of malting barley calls for great care in the control of water content, temperature and time allowed. Many other enzymes are produced including phytase, which helps to liberate the phosphorus compounds in the grain, the diastase enzymes, which will later convert the now readily available starch molecules into maltose, a compound of glucose molecules, and maltase, which can liberate the glucose from the maltose. Malting is an extremely complex operation and it is therefore very important for the home brewer, just as much as for the commercial brewer, to use only suitable barley that has been properly malted. The malt should always be bought from a reputable supplier and offers of cheap malt should always be ignored. The difference in cost is very slight compared with the difference in the beer produced. Good beer can be brewed only from good malt.

As soon as the seed has germinated, the maltster increases the warmth, dries out the grain and stops further growth. In this state the barley is now called pale malt. Slightly longer heating at a higher temperature darkens the grain a little and this is called crystal malt. Even longer heating and higher temperature produce chocolate and black malts. The former contains little fermentable carbohydrate but bestows flavour and a dark brown colour. The black malt imparts only flavour and colour. The malt is now completely caramelized but not carbonated and is used mostly in the making of stout.

It is clear, then, that in brewing it is

essential to use mostly pale malt with some crystal in bitter beers, and with some chocolate and black malts for brown ales and stouts. Some 75% of the weight of pale malt consists of fermentable sugars. Before being used, however, the pale malt must be crushed or coarsely ground to expose the starch, just as grapes and other fruits are crushed when making wine from them.

Malt Extract

The starch in the malted barley is converted into maltose by the diastase enzymes, alpha and beta amylase, while the crushed grains are being steeped in hot water. By controlling his blend of grains, the hardness and temperature of the liquor and the length of time of their infusion, or mashing as it is called, the brewer can produce different worts for the different styles of beer. That is why the same style of beer can vary from one brewery to another.

Having produced the wort some brewers now concentrate it into a toffee-like syrup of which about 80% is fermentable. Thus 500 g of malt extract is approximately equivalent to 400 g of sugar. This malt extract, or syrup, can be bought in different styles suitable for different beers, or with retained diastase to convert the starch of adjuncts to glucose. It is also marketed with hop flavourings ready to be diluted and fermented into beer. This is the well-known beer kit.

Malt Flour

Malt extract contains about 20% water, but this can be removed and the extract turned into a flour that is almost wholly fermentable. It is absolutely essential to keep this flour free from all moisture and humidity, otherwise some will be absorbed and the flour will set into a rock-hard lump that is very difficult to dissolve. The flour is available in three different colours – pale, medium and dark. You should use mostly pale malt flour, with just enough dark for colouring.

Average Extraction Guide

When formulating a recipe of your own, it is helpful to know the approximate quantity of fermentable sugar, expressed as units of specific gravity, contained in each ingredient. The following items are for 450 g/1 lb of ingredient dissolved or mashed in water to make a finished total of 4.5 litres/1 gallon.

Ingredient	Specific Gravity
White sugar	1.036
Brown sugar	1.034
Glucose chips	1.034
Golden syrup	1.028
Malt extract	1.028
Pale malt mashed	1.024
Crystal malt	1.020
Flaked rice/maize/barley	1.022
Black malt	1.000

With very accurate measurements and careful mashing where necessary, it is possible to attain slightly higher figures than those quoted. With the facilities available in most homes, however, those given are more realistic and are a useful guide when devising your own recipes.

The approximate alcohol content can be calculated by subtracting the specific gravity of the finished beer, just before priming, from the original gravity and multiplying the result by $\frac{3}{22}$.

Thus: original gravity   1.044
        final gravity $\underline{1.008}$
                                    36

$$36 \times \frac{3}{22} = \frac{54}{11} = \text{approx } 5\% \text{ alcohol}$$

Hops

The hop bine, *humulus lupulus*, has been around for thousands of years, but in Britain it has been used extensively only for the last 400 years. Previously ale was consumed without further flavouring, although sometimes herbs or fruits were added, yarrow, spruce and burdock being the most popular. The hops were brought over from the Continent by Huguenots, who settled in Kent and planted their bines there. The different strains were slowly improved, notably by a Mr Golding, who gave his name to a variety that proved to be most suitable for flavouring and preserving the different bitter beers produced from hard water. Similarly, a Mr Fuggle gave his name to a variety that proved to be most suitable for flavouring and preserving brown ales and stouts.

The bittering factor in hops is derived from the alpha acid, humulon, and the beta acid, lupulon, content. Research has been carried out, notably at the Wye institute of Agriculture in Kent, into the possibility of developing new hop strains with higher alpha acid contents. The higher the acid content, the fewer the hops that are needed, and this reduces transport and warehouse costs. As a result, Wye Challenger has now taken over from the Golding and Wye Northdown from the Fuggle. Another popular hop, Northern Brewer, has been succeeded by Wye Target. When any of the new varieties are being used up to 20 per cent fewer hops are needed: thus, 40 grams of Challenger is as effective as 50 grams of Goldings.

To assist the commercial breweries ways have now been found of concentrating the hop flower. The petals are ground up in a cold atmosphere and the unwanted particles of stalk and petal removed. The remainder is compressed into pellets, which are even cheaper to transport and store. The degree of concentration varies and must be taken into account when the pellets are used. They are especially useful for dry hopping – the addition of hops during fermentation to enhance the hop aroma. For this purpose only, concentrated hop oil may be used, but a few drops per gallon is sufficient.

The hop bine grows to a height of about four metres and is supported by a string attached to a wire frame. The flowers are borne towards the top and are harvested mechanically. Each flower, some two to three centimetres long, is shaped like a cone and consists of layers of yellow green petals attached to a stalk. At the base of the petals is a golden powder which contains the alpha and beta acids. The petals themselves contain essential oils that make them water repellent. When being used they must be squeezed in the water to make them absorb it and sink to the bottom. They would otherwise float on the surface of the wort and it would be impossible to extract the essential oils, acids and tannin. This is done by boiling the hops in the wort for up to one hour. The boil must be vigorous so that the hops are moved about by the bubbles of air and thus assist in the extraction. The length of boil varies the bitterness of the wort but a long boil reduces the fresh hop aroma. It is all a matter of taste, and dry hopping is only necessary if you like the hop flavour.

Water

Since 95% of beer is water, it is essential to use the best available. Fresh spring water is good, so is deep well water. Rainwater must be filtered and boiled and is extremely soft. Most of the tap water available in the United Kingdom is perfectly adequate, but if it contains chlorine it should first be boiled in an open pan for a few minutes to drive off the chlorine. Failure to do this will impart an unpleasant antiseptic taste to the beer.

In the mashing of grains the hardness or softness of the water plays a significant part. Hard water is most suitable for all the bitter beers and barley wine, while soft water produces better brown ales, stouts and lagers. Hardness is caused by the presence of a number of mineral salts, notably calcium carbonate, calcium sulphate, magnesium sulphate, calcium chloride and sodium chloride. The commercial brewer can adjust the water he uses for the different beers by the addition of a small quantity of these salts in different proportions. Stouts, for example, need more of the chloride and carbonate salts and almost none of the sulphates. Conversely, a Burton-type bitter needs relatively large quantities of calcium sulphate and only moderate quantities of the others. The home brewer can obtain an analysis of the water available to him and adjust it accordingly. Hardening salts may be purchased, if necessary, to add to soft water.

The effect of the hardness or softness of the water is most significant in the mashing of grains to produce the wort. It is of much less significance in the dilution of a ready-prepared malt extract. The presence of chlorine, however, is important and all of the water to be used for brewing should first be boiled and allowed to cool until required. Good liquor makes good beer and many of the 'off' flavours in home brews can be attributed to the water used. It is well worth taking the trouble to get this right.

Adjuncts

All ingredients other than malt, hops and liquor are known to the brewer as adjuncts. The most commonly used is sugar, which is the least expensive way of increasing the alcohol content of the beer. Sugar must be used with discretion, however, since too much would unbalance the beer. The sugar content of a brew should never produce more than one-third of the alcohol and preferably no more than one-quarter – the less the better. Household sugar in granulated form is the most widely used.

Because commercial brewers use invert sugar, some home brewers make their own invert sugar by boiling their household sugar in water with a little citric acid for twenty minutes. Two pounds of sugar, one level teaspoonful of citric acid and one pint of water produce two pints of invert sugar. Boiling the sugar in a weak acid solution splits the two molecules of glucose and fructose apart and enables the yeast to start reducing them to alcohol and carbon dioxide without first having to split the sucrose molecules into glucose and fructose. This is a short saving in time and risk for the commercial brewer but of no advantage to the home brewer making no more than five gallons at a time.

There is, however, a small advantage in using glucose in the form of crystallized lumps called chips, or as a white powder or a colourless syrup. The yeast enzymes ferment glucose more readily than fructose and a drier beer is produced. Golden syrup is sometimes used but it contains a little flavouring as well as invert sugar. Brown sugar may be used for the darker beers but this, too, contains a little flavouring. Black treacle may be employed as a colorant and one tablespoonful per gallon is usually enough. Honey should not be used unless you intend to make a honey beer, for the flavouring is significant.

Flakes

After sugar, flaked rice, flaked maize and flaked barley are the most popular adjuncts. Although the starch cells are broken during the flaking process, these grains contain no diastase enzymes. It follows that there must be an excess of these enzymes in the mash if these grains are to be used. If a full grain mash is being prepared there is no problem, but if a malt extract is being used, care should be taken to ensure that it contains diastase. Ordinary malt extract, available from chemists, is not likely to be suitable. A diastatic malt syrup, bought as such from a specialist shop supplying home brew ingredients and equipment, is recommended. Even so, the quantity of flakes used should not exceed 10% of the weight of the malt. They also have a tendency to diminish the head retention quality of a beer if used in a higher proportion. These flakes do have the advantage, however, of a low soluble nitrogen content and make the beer both easier to fine and more stable. They also impart a crisp flavour to the beer.

Other adjuncts included to vary the flavour of a beer are roasted barley which is unmalted and imparts a drier, less full flavour than black malt. It is widely used in the brewing of Irish-style stouts. Torrified barley adds some colour and body to a beer and gives a slightly nutty taste. A little may be used in beers similar in style to export ale. It should not, however, be used in light ales. Raw barley is sometimes used in bitter beers to impart a grainy taste.

Wheat in the form of flakes, flour or syrup may be used in the preparation of draught mild ales. Oats and rye are sometimes used but they add a very bitter flavour and should be employed only in very small quantities in stouts.

Yeast

This is the final ingredient without which beer cannot be made. This single-cell fungus contains within it all the enzymes necessary to convert maltose into alcohol and carbon dioxide. It is invisible to the naked eye and even when multiplied 500 times in size under a microscope looks no bigger than a pinhead. It is mostly available to the home brewer in the form of putty-coloured granules of dormant cells, which have to be activated before they can begin fermenting. This is best done by diluting a cupful of warm wort with a cupful of cold boiled water. Check the temperature with a culinary thermometer and, when the reading is between 40° and 45°C/104° and 113°F, sprinkle on the yeast granules. This temperature, as with all others in brewing, is quite important. Scientific research has shown that, within this narrow range, the dormant cells swell most quickly to their normal size with minimal loss of vitality. At a higher temperature the cells are likely to be destroyed. At a lower temperature they take longer to absorb the moisture and, in so doing, lose some of their essential constituents.

Once the granules have dissolved, the solution should be left for about 15 minutes, by when there will be a frothy mass on the surface and the activated yeast will be ready for pitching. Malt contains an adequate supply of nitrogen for the yeast cells and so the addition of an ammonium nutrient is not recommended.

Keep it clean

In the brewing of good beer few factors are more important than cleanliness. Although we cannot see them, millions of micro-organisms are floating in the air, settling on everything with which they come into contact. If there is the least trace of moisture they are held by it and soon begin to multiply. Left to come into contact with a beer, they impart a sour, bitter, ·or rotting vegetation taste to it. Vinegar bacteria in particular like to live in a beer and soon turn the alcohol into acetic acid.

Washing your equipment outside as well as inside is helpful in removing obvious dirty marks, but few surfaces, including glass, are so smooth as not to contain countless invisible caverns in which the bacteria, moulds, fungi and spores can live and thrive. After washing and rinsing the equipment should be sterilized before use.

The most effective sterilizing agent for home brewers is a white powder sold under the trade name of Chempro. It is a chlorine-based agent that dissolves quickly in water.

It is sufficient to make up a solution and use it to wash every surface that can come into contact with the wort or beer. Swirl it around the inside of a bin several times, fill a bottle and, after a few seconds, pour the solution into the next bottle. Leave crown caps in a small basinful of the solution for a short while, fill the siphon tube with it and the hydrometer trial jar with the hydrometer in it. Rinse out pressure kegs with it and soak nylon or calico sparging bags in it. Make a habit of never using unsterilized equipment and you will at once eradicate the most common cause of 'off' flavours.

But Chempro, like bleach or any other chlorine-based sterilizing agent, can also spoil a brew unless it is subsequently rinsed off with running cold water. Chlorine in water reacts with the phenolics in hops to form trichlorophenol, more commonly known as T.C.P., and with the same unpleasant smell and taste. After sterilizing with Chempro, wash out each item in plenty of cold water, and then smell it to make sure that it is clean.

An alternative to Chempro is sulphite, another white powder, more precisely called sodium metabisulphite. It is also available in the form of Campden tablets. When it is dissolved in water sulphurous acid is formed and the sulphur element sterilizes the surfaces with which it comes into contact. The sulphur is a little less potent than the chlorine, although it can be reinforced with citric acid, but it does have the advantage of not needing to be washed off. It is sufficient to drain off the surplus moisture and use the equipment immediately. After use every piece of equipment should be washed, dried and put away in a dry place, but should be sterilized again immediately prior to use the next time.

Ingredients should not be sterilized with Chempro, sulphite or any other agent. The boiling process takes good care of the micro-organisms and kills them all. After boiling, however, it is very important to keep the wort covered to protect it from fresh organisms floating in the air that may fall into it. Most fermentation bins are supplied with fitting lids, but failing this, a sheet of plastic fastened with a piece of elastic would do, or just a thick cloth. Muslin and nylon are not suitable.

The fermenting beer throws up a cloud of carbon dioxide that is heavier than air. It lies on the surface of the wort and so helps to protect it from infection. Keeping the wort and finished beer protected from the air is as important as sterilizing the equipment.

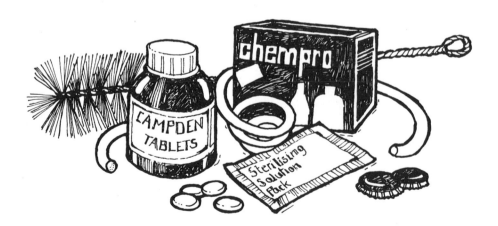

Kit beers

Undoubtedly the fastest way to make beer is with a so-called 'kit'. There are two kinds – wet and dry. The wet is made from malt extract flavoured with hop oils, and the dry is made from malt flour, some grains and hops. Different styles of beer are available in both kinds and in different quantities.

The most popular is the wet kit for making bitter beer. The kit consists of a container – usually a can – full of toffee-like malt extract, coloured and flavoured to produce a bitter-style beer. A sachet of yeast granules is usually supplied, together with full instructions on how to make the beer. All the home brewer has to provide is some sugar, the water, a fermentation bin and bottles.

First, the bin must be sterilized with a sulphite solution; then some warm water is poured into it. The container is opened and emptied into the water, which must be stirred well to dissolve the malt. The container should be rinsed out with some more warm water so that no malt is wasted. Some manufacturers then recommend the boiling of the wort for five minutes, but others regard this as unnecessary. Nevertheless, it is better to follow the instructions. The sugar is then stirred in and the cold water is added to make the total quantity up to that prescribed for the amount of malt used. The temperature of the wort is checked and, at about 24°C/75°F, the yeast is stirred in. Fermentation soon follows and continues for four or five days. The beer is then ready for bottling, priming and sealing. After another four or five days the beer is just mature enough for drinking, but it will improve if kept for a week or two longer.

Some of the instructions suggest using less water than that recommended to obtain a slightly stronger and more full-bodied beer. These adjustments are a matter of taste and much depends on your palate and your discernment of the finer qualities of a beer. Wet kits are widely available from home brew shops, Boots the Chemist, Woolworths, some supermarkets, do-it-yourself centres, gardening centres and so on. Several millions of people make them regularly or from time to time and are well satisfied with the results. They are, certainly, the best way for anyone new to brewing to get to know the simple technique.

The concentrates may vary slightly in flavour from one manufacturer to another, depending on the grains he selects for his mash, the water he uses, the temperature at which he mashes and for how long. Other variable factors are the quality and variety of hops or isomerized hop oil chosen, the length of the boil, the clarification of the wort and the final concentration. Every variation will produce a marginally different kit. In the beginning it is worth making up a number of the same style of kits from different manufacturers so that you can see which one you like best. No one can tell you which is the best. You have to decide for yourself from the taste of the one you enjoy most.

Having found their favourite brew, many people venture no further and make up a kit every week or so, depending on their drinking habits. The beer can be casked as well as bottled and, after making a few brews, the whole process becomes a quick and simple routine.

Making up a dry kit is very similar except that an hour's boiling is involved. The hops and grains are packed in a muslin bag which you are recommended to boil for one hour in a prescribed quantity of water. There is a strong belief, however, that a better extraction rate can be achieved by emptying the contents of the bag in the water and allowing the grains and hops to be moved around freely by the boiling. The slight disadvantage is in straining out the solids. If the grains and hops are left in the muslin bag they can be more easily removed when the boiling is finished. While the boiling is in process, the malt flour and sugar are dissolved in a bin ready for the hops and grain liquor. The rest of the process is the same as that described for a wet kit.

Malt extract and hop beers

If the kits fail to produce exactly the taste and flavour that you are looking for, then you should brew from malt extract and hops. You can buy malt extract suitably prepared for making bitter, lager and stout, usually in cans containing from 450 g/1 lb up to 1.8 kg/4 lb and occasionally even larger quantities. You can add hops and liquor, and adjuncts, including sugar, to suit yourself. Remember not to use too many adjuncts or too much sugar.

You can make changes to the brews by using other kinds of hops, boiling them for varying lengths of time, adding some fresh (or different) hops for the last quarter of an hour, or dry hop with pellets. Vary the quantity of water you use and the quantity of sugar. Use a diastatic malt syrup and a few flakes or some crushed crystal malt grains. Keep a note of your experiments so that when you produce a beer that you think is quite superb, you can reproduce it regularly.

Experimental brews are great fun and, although you may make some that you enjoy a little more than others, you will find them all attractive in different ways. The great secret is not to use too much of any adjunct and not to make the beers too strong. An original gravity of around 1.044 produces a strong enough beer for regular drinking. At first it is better to brew in the lower 40s rather than the upper 40s. The fermentation is likely to finish with a specific gravity around 1.008 or just below, depending on how much sugar was included. The more sugar you use the lower is likely to be the finished specific gravity and the thinner the beer. The higher gravity figure comes from

the difficult-to-ferment dextrins, which give body and a hint of sweetness to the beer.

A number of examples are given to guide you rather than for you to emulate. What suits one person may not suit another but, when carefully made, the following recipes produce good beers.

Bitter Beer   Original Gravity 1.042

(Illustrated sequence overleaf)

Malt extract	900 g/2 lb
Sugar	340 g/12 oz
Golding hops	35 g/1¼ oz
Water to	9 l/2 gall
Beer yeast	

Boil all but a handful of hops in one gallon of water in a covered pan for 45 minutes (1). Remove from the heat and leave for five minutes while the hops settle. Strain into a bin, pressing the hops before discarding them (2). Stir in the malt extract and sugar (3) and when they are dissolved return the wort to the pan and simmer for a further five minutes (4). Empty into a fermentation bin and add cold water to bring the quantity up to the 9-litre/2-gallon mark. Remove half a cup of hot wort and empty it into a large jug containing a cup of cold boiled water (5 and 6). Stir well to admit some air, adjust the temperature to 40°C/104°F (7), then sprinkle on the yeast granules. Check the temperature of the wort and as soon as it is down to around 21°C/70°F, pitch the activated yeast (8), stir well and then loosely cover the bin with its lid or a thick cloth (9).

1

2

3

4

5

6

7

8

Next day, skim off any scum from the surface of the wort (**10**), wipe the dead yeast and hop particles from the side of the bin level with the surface of the wort, then stir well and re-cover the bin (**11**). Repeat this process on the following day but, before replacing the lid, add the rest of the hops, wetting them so that they do not float on the surface.

Leave the beer to finish fermenting, usually on the fifth or sixth day. Then move it to as cold a place as you can find for 48 hours to encourage as many solid particles as possible to settle down on the bottom of the bin (**12**). Take out half a cupful of the beer and dissolve in it eight level five-millilitre (5 ml) spoonsful of sugar – neither more nor less (**13**). Distribute this evenly between 16 sterilized one-pint beer bottles, then siphon the beer into the bottom of each bottle and fill to within five centimetres/two inches of the top (**14**). This figure is again important, as it leaves room for the gas pressure to build up. By placing the end of the siphon tube beneath the level of the beer in the bottle frothing is minimized.

Seal the bottles with sterilized screw stoppers or crown caps (**15**), then shake each one gently and listen for a hissing sound, which indicates an imperfect seal that must be replaced. Leave the bottles in a warm room for a few days while the priming sugar is fermented. Then store them in a cooler place for ten days or so. Within 21 days of starting the brew you will have some real ale that you can hardly fail to enjoy.

Variation 1

Diastatic malt syrup	900 g/2 lb
Flaked rice	100 g/3½ oz
Golding hops	35 g/1¼ oz
Water to	9 l/2 gall
Sugar	280 g/10 oz
Beer yeast	

Dissolve the malt in 2 litres/3½ pints of hot water (75°C/167°F), stir in the flaked rice, cover and leave for 45 minutes. Strain out the rice, mix in the hop liquor (prepared as described above), simmer for five minutes and then continue as described above.

Variation 2

Diastatic malt syrup	900 g/2 lb
Flaked maize	100 g/3½ oz
Golding hops	35 g/1¼ oz
Water to	9 l/2 gall
Sugar	280 g/10 oz
Beer yeast	

Brew as just described in Variation 1.

Variation 3

Malt extract	900 g/2 lb
Crushed crystal malt	100 g/3½ oz
Golding hops	35 g/1¼ oz
Water to	9 l/2 gall
Sugar	280 g/10 oz
Beer yeast	

Brew as described in Variation 1.

Variation 4

Malt extract	900 g/2 lb
Golding hops	28 g/1 oz
Northern Brewer hops	7 g/¼ oz
Water to	9 l/2 gall
Sugar	340 g/12 oz
Beer yeast	

Boil all the Golding hops for 45 minutes, add the Northern Brewer hops and continue to boil for a further 15 minutes. Leave for five minutes while the hops settle, then strain out the hops, stir in the malt extract and continue as described in the basic recipe, except for the dry hopping which is omitted.

Variation 5

Malt extract	900 g/2 lb
Golding hops	28 g/1 oz
Northern Brewer hops	7 g/¼ oz
Water to	9 l/2 gall
Golden syrup	450 g/1 lb
Beer yeast	

Brew as described in the basic recipe.

Variation 5a, 5b, 5c, 5d.

Use 450 g/1 lb golden syrup instead of sugar in Variations 1, 2, 3, and 4.

Variation 6

Diastatic malt syrup	*450 g/1 lb*
Crushed pale malt	*450 g/1 lb*
Crushed crystal malt	*100 g/3½ oz*
Hard water to	*9 l/2 gall*
Wye Challenger hops	*28 g/1 oz*
Glucose chips	*340 g/12 oz*
Beer yeast	

Dissolve the malt extract in 3 litres/5 pints of hot water (75°C/167°F), stir in the crushed pale and crystal malts, cover with a thick blanket and leave for one and a half hours. Strain out the grains and wash them twice in one litre/two pints of hot water each time. Add all the hops and boil for one hour. Leave for 20 minutes while the solids settle.

Strain through a nylon bag and, when all the liquor has drained off, rinse the hops with one pint of hot water (75°C/167°F) poured slowly over them. When this has drained through repeat the process, by which time the hops should be free of all sugar and may be discarded. Stir the glucose chips into the wort and, when it is dissolved, top up with cold water. As soon as the temperature falls to 20°C/68°F pitch an active yeast and continue brewing as already described.

Variation 7a

Diastatic malt syrup	*450 g/1 lb*
Crushed pale malt	*340 g/12 oz*
Flaked maize	*110 g/4 oz*
Hard water to	*9 l/2 gall*
Wye Challenger hops	*28 g/1 oz*
Glucose chips	*340 g/12 oz*
Beer yeast	

Brew as in Variation 6.

Variation 7b

Diastatic malt syrup	*450 g/1 lb*
Crushed pale malt	*340 g/12 oz*
Flaked rice	*110 g/4 oz*
Hard water to	*9 l/2 gall*
Wye Challenger hops	*28 g/1 oz*
Glucose chips	*340 g/12 oz*
Beer yeast	

Brew as already described in Variation 6.

Other Beers

The basic recipe can also be varied to produce export ales, light ales, brown ales and stouts.

Export Ale   Original Gravity 1.053

Diastatic malt syrup	*900 g/2 lb*
Crystal malt	*100 g/3½ oz*
Flaked maize	*100 g/3½ oz*
Torrified barley	*100 g/3½ oz*
Light brown sugar	*450 g/1 lb*
Wye Challenger hops	*28 g/1 oz*
Wye Target hops	*7 g/¼ oz*
Hard water to	*9 l/2 gall*
Juice of half a lemon	
Beer yeast	

Dissolve the malt extract in 4 litres/7 pints of hot water, and stir in the crystal malt, flaked maize, torrified barley and Challenger hops. Bring to the boil in a covered pan and maintain a rolling boil for 45 minutes. Mix in the Wye Target hops, pushing them down with a plastic paddle. Stir in the sugar and lemon juice and continue to boil for a further 15 minutes; then leave to cool for 30 minutes.

Strain out the solids through a fine-meshed nylon bag and slowly spray 2 litres/3½ pints of hot water over them to remove all traces of sugar. Squeeze the bag as a final gesture before discarding the contents. Top up with cold water and, when cool, pitch an activated yeast. Skim, stir, prime, seal and store as described in the basic recipe. The beer benefits from slightly longer storage since it is strong and full-flavoured.

Variation

Three-quarters of the light brown sugar could be replaced with 450 g/1 lb golden syrup and the lemon juice then omitted. Its presence in the recipe converts the sugar to glucose and fructose during the boiling and so ensures a rapid fermentation. The lemon juice also ensures a slightly acidic wort in which the yeast prefers to ferment. If your tap water is particularly chalky, it is an advantage to add half a lemon or a teaspoonful of citric acid per gallon.

Light Ale Original Gravity 1.037

Light malt extract	*900 g/2 lb*
Flaked maize	*100 g/3½ oz*
Glucose chips	*200 g/7 oz*
Hallertau hops	*28 g/1 oz*
Hard water to	*9 l/2 gall*
Beer yeast	

Boil the flaked maize and the hops in a covered pan for one hour. Strain into a bin, rinse the hops and maize with a little hot water, stir in the malt extract and glucose, top up with cold water and, when cool, pitch an activated yeast. Skim, stir, prime, seal and store as described in the basic recipe.

Brown Ale Original Gravity 1.028

Malt extract	*900 g/2 lb*
Chocolate malt	*125 g/4½ oz*
Black malt	*50 g/1¾ oz*
Wye Northdown hops	*28 g/1 oz*
Soft water to	*9 l/2 gall*
Beer yeast	

Boil the hops and grains in a covered pan for one hour, strain them out and stir in the malt extract, and then simmer for five minutes. Top up with cold water and, when cool, pitch an activated yeast. No additional sugar is required. Skim, stir, prime, seal and store as described in the basic recipe.

This is a 'dry' brown ale. If a slightly sweeter version is preferred, mix in 100 g/3½ oz lactose with the malt extract. If you prefer a less dark brown ale, omit the black malt.

Stout (Dry) Original Gravity 1.042

Malt extract	*900 g/2 lb*
Crystal malt	*250 g/9 oz*
Flaked maize	*100 g/3½ oz*
Black malt	*100 g/3½ oz*
Brown sugar	*340 g/12 oz*
Juice of half a lemon	
Wye Northdown hops	*50 g/1¾ oz*
Soft water to	*9 l/2 gall*
Stout yeast	

Dissolve the malt extract in hot water, stir in the flaked maize, crystal malt grains, whole black malt grains, brown sugar, lemon juice and all but a handful of hops, wetting them thoroughly. Boil in a covered pan for one hour, leave for 10 minutes while the solids settle, and then strain through a fine-meshed nylon bag. Rinse the hops and grains with hot water to remove the final traces of sugar, then discard them. Top up with cold water and, when cool, pitch an active yeast. Skim and stir for two days, then dry hop with the handful reserved from the boiling. Finish the fermentation, rack, prime, seal and store as in the basic recipe. This beer improves with longer storage.

Stout (Sweet) Original Gravity 1.034

Malt extract	*900 g/2 lb*
Crystal malt	*250 g/9 oz*
Black malt	*100 g/3½ oz*
Wye Northdown hops	*35 g/1¼ oz*
Soft water to	*9 l/2 gall*
Stout yeast	
Lactose	*100 g/3½ oz*

Make in the same way as just described for a dry stout. Add the lactose after the boiling stage. Sweet stout is always less strong than dry stout. If it is not sweet enough for you add more lactose.

Barley Wine   Original Gravity 1.088

Diastatic malt syrup	*900 g/2 lb*
Crushed pale malt	*250 g/9 oz*
Crushed crystal malt	*250 g/9 oz*
Brown sugar	*125 g/4½ oz*
Juice of half a lemon	
Golding hops	*28 g/1 oz*
Hard water to	*4.5 l/1 gall*
Champagne wine yeast	

Heat 2 litres/3½ pints water to 75°C/167°F and stir in the malt syrup, crushed pale malt and crystal malt. Cover closely with a blanket to keep in the warmth and leave for one hour. Strain out the grains and sparge them slowly with 2 litres/3½ pints of hot water. Stir in the brown sugar, lemon juice and the hops and boil the wort in a covered pan for one hour. Remove from the heat and leave for 15 minutes while the solids settle.

Strain through a fine-meshed nylon bag and slowly spray with half a litre/1 pint of hot water, and press the solids dry before discarding them. Top up with cold water to the one-gallon level. Remove 100 ml/3½ fl oz of wort and dilute with an equal quantity of cold water. When the temperature is 40°C/104°F, mix in the champagne wine yeast and leave it to regenerate for about 15 minutes. Also remove a second 100 ml/3½ fl oz of wort and store in a well-sealed bottle in the refrigerator until the beer is ready for bottling. When the rest of the wort has cooled to 20°C/68°F, pitch the now active wine yeast, stir well, and then cover the bin and leave for 24 hours.

By this time the tumultuous ferment should be over. The wort should be stirred again and then poured into a fermentation jar. If the tumultuous ferment is still in progress, that is, if there is a mass of frothy bubbles on the wort, leave it in the bin for a day or so before transferring the wort to the jar. Champagne wine yeast ferments from the bottom and usually throws little froth. Fit an airlock and leave the jar in an even temperature until fermentation is finished. Move the jar to a cold place for a few days to encourage the beer to clear. If you wish, finings may be added but this is rarely necessary.

Siphon the clear beer into 16 half-pint bottles, prime each one with an equal portion of the reserved wort from the refrigerator. Seal each bottle perfectly, label and store for one week in a warm place and for one year in a cool store. Serve in wine goblets.

Lager   Original Gravity 1.045

Malt extract for lager	*900 g/2 lb*
Crushed pale lager malt	*250 g/9 oz*
Flaked barley	*200 g/7 oz*
Glucose chips	*200 g/7 oz*
Hallertau hops	*35 g/1¼ oz*
Soft water to	*9 l/2 gall*
Carlsberg yeast	

Dissolve the malt extract in warm water (60°C/140°F) in a boiling pan. Stir in the crushed pale malt and flaked barley. Cover and leave for 30 minutes. Place the pan on the stove and increase the temperature of the wort to 67°C/154°F. Remove from the heat, replace the cover and leave for a further 30 minutes.

Add the hops, wetting them thoroughly, then bring to the boil and maintain this for 45 minutes. Remove from the heat, leave for 15 minutes, then strain out and rinse the solids, stir in the glucose, top up with cold water and, when the temperature falls to 20°C/68°F, pitch an activated Carlsberg yeast. Stir well, cover, and leave for 24 hours.

Pour into two demijohns, fit airlocks and leave the wort to ferment out in a cool place, 10° to 15°C/50° to 59°F. A long, slow fermentation is desirable. When the lager is clear, siphon it into bottles, prime in the usual way, then seal and store for three months. Serve it cold.

Grain-mashed beers

When mashing grains for beer a number of factors are of equal importance. Error in any of them will affect the quality of the finished beer. Buy only the best ingredients you can get. Buy them from a busy centre where fresh goods are constantly coming into stock.

Hops

Make sure that they have a fresh lime-green colour. Rub a few loose hops between the palms of your hands and be certain, when you smell them, that they have a pronounced and fresh aroma. Select your variety from sealed packets of compressed whole hops. Avoid fading hops in thin polythene bags. Hop pellets should be sealed in foil or in vapour-proof polythene.

Malt

If possible, buy your malted grains already crushed and sealed in a thick polythene bag. Otherwise, bite a malt grain between your teeth to ensure that it tastes crisp and biscuity. If you have to crush the grains yourself, put them through a coarse mincer or give them a few seconds in a coffee grinder or the like. Be careful not to overdo this. You need to crush or crack the grains rather than grind them to a flour. An alternative method is to soak the grains in cold water for an hour and then to crush them between a rolling pin and a formica surface. Black malt needs no crushing.

Pale malt grains should always constitute the bulk of your mash. It is from these that the major part of the malt sugar must come. Mashed in one gallon of liquor (adjusted water), 1 lb of crushed malt grains should produce a specific gravity of approximately 1.024. In theory you should achieve a higher figure. In practice calculate on 1.024 and you won't be far out. Crystal malt and flakes produce rather less, around 1.021, but chocolate and black grains contribute nothing except colour and flavour.

Adjuncts

Blending the grist is the next consideration. If too large a quantity of flakes or other adjuncts is included the beer will lose much of its malty flavour. Adjuncts are included mainly to economize on the quantity of malt required but also to enhance or vary the flavour, to increase the body of the beer and to assist in head retention. A good mash should not contain adjuncts in excess of one-fifth of the total quantity of malt. An even better mash would contain as little as one-eighth. Flakes need no crushing or grinding before use. The process of flaking the grain makes the starch readily available to the diastase enzymes. Always mash the adjuncts with the malts.

Liquor

Most people have water of excellent quality flowing from their taps. An analysis can be obtained from your local water board so that you know how to adjust it for making the different styles of beer. Only tiny quantities of mineral salts are required and the figures in the table below are given for a five-gallon brew.

The figures represent grains, the chemist's method of measuring minute quantities. One gram is equivalent to 15 grains. One ounce is approximately equal to 425 grains. If you are preparing the mixture yourself, make a larger quantity, say enough for 50 gallons, and use only one-tenth at a time for a five-gallon brew. But obtain the local water analysis first.

Temperature

The temperature of the liquor is the next important factor. Because the crushed malt grains have to be stirred into the liquor, a slightly higher striking temperature is necessary to allow for the loss of heat in stirring. 75°C/167°F is a suitable temperature for the liquor at the time of stirring in the pale malt and adjuncts for bitter beer. A lower temperature is needed for other beers. By the time this process is completed the temperature will have fallen by about 8°C/15°F. Every effort should be made to maintain the recommended mashing temperature, especially for the first half hour. The container should be closely covered and insulated as best you can. (*See* the chapter *The Things You Need*.)

Mashing

After half an hour the mash needs a good stir to help extract the starch from the grist. The liquor may also need a little hot water to restore the temperature. Half a pint of boiling water will restore a gallon of wort at 64.7°C/148.5°F to 66.7°C/152°F. One pint will raise a gallon of wort from 62.5°C/144.5°F back to 66.7°C/152°F. The hot water must be stirred in to distribute the heat evenly.

The quantity of liquor used is also important. If the mash is too thick, the extraction will be insufficient. If it is too thin, too much albuminous and unconverted starch will be extracted. As a rough guide, reckon to mash between 3 and 4 lb of grist in one gallon of water, and sparge with at least another half-gallon at the striking temperature. As your experience grows you will find more precise figures relative to the grist you use, the nature of the water, the temperature at which you mash, the ability of your equipment to maintain an even temperature, the length of your mash and your sparging facilities.

After the stirring and any increase in heat that may be necessary the mash may be left, well-covered and insulated, until conversion is finished – a period of about two hours.

End Point

To test that the end point has been reached and that all the starch has been converted to maltose and dextrin, remove a tablespoonful

	Light Ales	Pale Ales	Best Bitter	Barley Wine	Stouts and Brown Ales	Lager
Calcium Sulphate	50–75	75–125	200–250	250	—	—
Magnesium Sulphate	10–20	20–30	20–30	30	10	—
Calcium Chloride	30–40	10–20	20–30	30	25–50	30–50
Sodium Chloride	40–50	20–30	20–30	25	75–100	80–100
Calcium Carbonate	10	10	10	10	40–60	40

or two of the wort and place it in the centre of a white saucer. Add a few drops of household iodine and, if the wort turns blue or darkens, then some starch remains unconverted and mashing should continue. If there is no colour change then the wort is ready for the next stage.

Sparging

Drain off the wort and as soon as the grains have settled down, sparge them with a fine spray of hot water at the striking temperature – 75°C/167°F for bitter beers. Sparging effectively is not easy to achieve in the home and each home brewer works out the method most suitable to the facilities available. Some use a watering-can rose, others a shower head, others a pressurized garden spray kept exclusively for brewing and never, never used for spraying plants with insecticide, fungicide or fertilizer. The rose and shower head rarely produce more than a few large drops at a time unless held high. If you cannot justify an additional garden spray you will find that the narrow spout of an indoor-plant watering vessel is reasonably effective. Move the fine spout slowly over the grains, endeavouring to cover the entire surface as often as you can.

Should you have to use a mashing bin without a perforated bottom and a draw-off tap, pour the mash from the bin into a strong calico sparging bag suspended over a receiving vessel. The bag should be supported by a wire frame or in some other suitable way.

The sparging leaches out from the grains the maltose produced by the conversion of the starch during the mashing that is not already dissolved in the wort. When the first wort from the sparging comes through the grains it is well worthwhile checking its specific gravity. The first test often reveals quite a lot of maltose. When a subsequent test shows a reading of 1.002 or very nearly there, stop sparging and discard the grist. Check the specific gravity of the wort by rapidly cooling a full trial jar and making any necessary adjustments to temperature and quantity. Remember that a reading of 1.072 in one gallon is the same as 1.024 when the wort has been increased to 3 gallons with cold water.

Boiling

The hops of your choice should now be mixed into the wort. Mix them thoroughly by squeezing them with your hand so that they absorb the wort and sink to the bottom of the pan. This is a messy business because loose petals stick to your hands with the sugary wort, but it is a necessary process. If you wish, some carragheen moss may be added to assist in fining the wort. It can be put in with the hops or later in the boiling. Some hops may be reserved for adding towards the end of the boil.

A long vigorous boil is necessary to extract the tannin from the hops and to assist in the precipitation of the nitrogenous protein from the malt. The fresh hop flavour is then diminished: hence the addition of some hops towards the end of the boil which should last for one hour. The rolling boil is necessary so that the large bubbles of air can move the hops around in the wort and effect an efficient extraction.

Keep the pan covered during the boil to minimize loss of flavouring and to prevent the spreading of an odour which tends to hang about the house for some hours afterwards. Keeping the pan covered also increases the pressure and less heat is needed to effect a rolling boil. Care should be taken not to let the wort boil over. The pan should, therefore, not be overfilled. When the boiling is finished, leave the wort in as cool a place as you can find for up to half an hour while the hops settle down. For example, place the pan in a sink and let cold water flow over it slowly, absorbing the heat as it passes.

Strain out the hops and press them to remove any wort they may be holding before throwing them on to the rose bed in the garden. Stir into the wort any sugar required and top up with cold, liquor-adjusted water. Add about a third of a pint to half a pint more than required to allow for wastage when racking. It is also useful to check the pH of the wort – the acidity – and this can best be done with a pH indicator paper in the upper range from 4 to 7. A reading of from pH 5 to 5.5 is needed and, if the water from your tap contains a good deal of calcium carbonate, i.e., if your kettle furs up quickly, then add a small amount of citric acid to your must. A quarter of a teaspoonful to a gallon is usually sufficient.

Make sure that you have left some head-room in the bin to allow for frothing and for carrying the bin from one place to another. Now cover it and leave it to cool as quickly as possible but check the temperature from time to time. When 20°C/68°F is reached pitch an activated yeast.

Yeasting

A few home brewers may have brewery contacts and be able to obtain a pot of fresh brewer's yeast for their wort. Most of us have to use dried yeast granules and these should be activated before adding them to the wort.

Remove a cupful of wort and dilute it with another cupful of cold liquor. Check the temperature and adjust it to 42°C/108°F by cooling or warming the wort. At the right temperature sprinkle on the granules and cover the jug or other container with a cloth or plate. Leave it in a warm position for 15 minutes while the yeast cells are regenerated. We commonly use the top-fermenting yeast, *saccharomyces cerevisiae*, but for lager the bottom-fermenting yeast, *saccharomyces Carlsbergensis*, should be used. There is no reason why this yeast should not also be used for light and pale ales. For barley wines the normal beer yeast may be used but the inclusion of some champagne wine yeast ensures a good fermentation of the glucose. Malted barley contains a high proportion of nitrogen, so it is not necessary to add any ammonium salts as you do when making wine. Indeed, the wort benefits from the inclusion of a small quantity of adjuncts to absorb some of the excess nitrogen in the malt.

Before pitching the yeast and, as soon as the wort reaches a suitable temperature,

check the specific gravity and record the reading, now known as the original gravity. It is helpful to have this piece of information when preparing future brews, but in particular for comparing with the gravity of the beer when fermentation is finished. From the difference between the two figures you can quickly calculate the approximate alcohol content of the beer. Provided the yeast is vigorously activated it may now be mixed into the wort. This should be accompanied by a thorough stirring up of the wort to admit some oxygen from the air. Boiling drives off the oxygen, but the yeast needs oxygen to create a large colony for quick conversion of the sugars to alcohol.

The bin should now be loosely covered either with its lid or with a clean cloth. A substantial quantity of carbon dioxide will be given off during the fermentation and this must be allowed to escape into the atmosphere. If a tight-fitting lid is used, the gas may not be able to escape and the carbon dioxide could stop the activity of the yeast and cause a stuck ferment. The carbon dioxide is heavier than the air and so forms a barrier between the air and the wort.

Skimming

More froth is likely to be caused during the first few days' fermentation of a grain-mashed wort than of a malt extract wort. It will look quite solid and very uneven, and will develop within 24 hours unless you have a problem (*see* pages 56–7). It is called a rocky head and must be skimmed off and discarded. It contains millions of dead yeast cells and minute particles of grain and hop debris. At the same time, wipe away with a paper towel the dark ring around the bin at the surface of the wort. Then give the beer a good rousing, lifting up the wort from the bottom to the top so that it can absorb some oxygen after releasing any bound carbon dioxide. Re-cover the bin and leave for another 24 hours.

The frothy head will again be substantial but now it will be in more even lumps that brewers call a cauliflower head because of its resemblance to that vegetable. But this must be removed, the ring of dead yeast wiped away again and the wort thoroughly roused once more.

Dry Hopping

This is the moment for the addition of a small handful of hops, a few hop pellets or a few drops of hop oil per gallon. Don't add too much or you will create too strong a hop aroma and flavour. On the other hand, a few fresh hops or two or three hop pellets per gallon do give a nice tang to the beer. It depends to a large extent on how you like your beer: strongly flavoured with hops, mildly flavoured or somewhere in between. Replace the lid or cover and leave undisturbed for the fermentation to finish. Should you decide to look next day, you will see a smooth, thin skin of froth called a seal. Over the following two or three days this will separate from the sides of the bin, becoming smaller and smaller in the centre of the wort until it finally disappears. Fermentation is now finished and the beer is ready for removal from the sediment at the bottom of the bin.

Final Stages

The process of racking and that of bottling or casking, priming, sealing and storing is the same as for all other beers and has already been fully described on page 36. In general, grain-mashed beers, especially the stronger versions, take longer to mature than kit beers and some malt-extract and hop beers. Three months is often necessary for some bottled beers, but these splendid ales will keep for a year and still be superb to drink.

Krausening

Instead of priming with sugar or syrup, good brewers reserve some of the original wort for this purpose. After checking the original gravity, but before the activated yeast is pitched, withdraw a portion of the wort. Just how much to withdraw depends on the sweetness of the wort. Up to S.G. 1.040 you need to withdraw about 5%. In a five-gallon brew that is 2 pints of wort. Above S.G. 1.040 it is sufficient to withdraw about 4%. In a five-gallon brew this is between $1\frac{3}{4}$ pints and $1\frac{1}{2}$ pints. The sweeter the wort the smaller the quantity needed. So, for a reading of 1.046, then, $1\frac{3}{4}$ pints is needed, while for one of 1.052, $1\frac{1}{2}$ pints will be sufficient.

The withdrawn wort should be stored in a sealed bottle in a refrigerator until it is required for priming. It is important that the bottle is sterile and that it is stored in a cold place. When the beer is fully fermented and about to be casked or bottled, the reserved wort that has not been fermented is taken from the refrigerator and poured out of the bottle into the beer to be stored, the sugar in the wort acting as the primer for the beer. No additional sugar is required in these circumstances. Krausening is very effective with grain-mashed beers, especially if you want your beer to possess and retain a good head.

Records

Everyone who brews from grains should keep a detailed record of the ingredients used, the method followed, including mashing time and temperature, together with an evaluation of the beer. Record cards and holders may be bought, but an ordinary postcard or notebook will do. The more details you record the better. In particular, you need to get a fairly accurate record of your extraction from the malt and adjuncts that you use and how this varies with the mashing temperature, length of mash and sparging. This is the kind of information that will most help you to improve your methods and enable you to make even better beers in future.

Recipes

The following recipes have each been formulated to make 20 pints. More or less can be made by adjusting all the quantities proportionally, i.e., for 5 gallons just double the quantity of every ingredient except the yeast. The figure of 20 pints has been chosen because the quantity of wort fits comfortably into a 15-litre fermentation vessel. When it contains 20 pints of wort the weight of the bin will be around 28 lb – not too heavy to move safely without spilling. The 20 pints of beer produced is a reasonable quantity to bottle and store at a time.

Mild Ale

Pale malt	*1 kg/2¼ lb*
Crystal malt	*500 g/18 oz*
Brown sugar	*250 g/9 oz*
Northdown hops	*35 g/1¼ oz*
Medium soft water	*11 l/2½ gall*
Beer yeast	

Hard water can be adequately softened with half a teaspoonful of table salt. Heat one gallon to 70°C/158°F and stir in the crushed malt. Maintain 65°C/149°F to end point. Sparge slowly with half a gallon of water at 70°C, then boil the hops and wort for one hour. Leave to cool for 20 minutes, strain into a 15-litre bin, stir in the sugar until it is dissolved, top up with cold water, cover and leave to cool.

When the temperature falls to 20°C/68°F, pitch an active yeast, then ferment, skim, rouse-up, leave to clear, rack into beer bottles, prime, seal and store as already indicated.

Mild and Bitter

This is frequently achieved by blending two finished beers but it can be produced direct.

Pale malt	*1.125 kg/2½ lb*
Crystal malt	*375 g/13 oz*
Flaked rice	*285 g/10 oz*
Brown sugar	*200 g/7 oz*
Northdown hops	*28 g/1 oz*
Challenger hops	*14 g/½ oz*
Medium hard water	*11 l/2½ gall*
Beer yeast	

Very hard water should be softened with just a little salt. Very soft water should be treated with a half dose of hardening salts. Brew as described for mild ale, but add the Challenger hops only for the last 15 minutes of the boil.

Light Ale (1)

Pale malt	*1.125 kg/2½ lb*
Crystal malt	*125 g/4½ oz*
Flaked barley	*200 g/7 oz*
White sugar	*250 g/9 oz*
Citric acid	*2.5 g/½ tsp*
Challenger hops	*42 g/1½ oz*
Hard water	*11 l/2½ gall*
Beer yeast	

Heat one gallon of water to 73°C/164°F, then stir in the crushed malts and the flaked barley. Maintain 66°C/150°F to end point. Sparge with half a gallon of water at 73°C/164°F. Stir in the sugar and acid then boil with all but a handful of the hops for 45 minutes. Leave to cool for 30 minutes, then strain out the hops, top up with cold water, cover and leave to cool.

Pitch an active yeast at 20°C/68°F and, if possible, ferment at 17°C/63°F. After the second skimming and rousing, add the remaining hops and ferment out. Rack, bottle, prime and store as already described. Keep for two weeks and serve cool.

Light Ale (2)

Pale malt	*1.125 kg/2½ lb*
Flaked maize	*200 g/7 oz*
Golden syrup	*450 g/1 lb*
Hallertau hops	*50 g/1¾ oz*
Hard water	*11 l/2½ gall*
Beer yeast	

Brew as described for Light Ale (1), adding the syrup after boiling, when the hops have been strained out.

Light Ale (3)

Pale malt	*1.125 kg/2½ lb*
Flaked barley	*200 g/7 oz*
Golden syrup	*450 g/1 lb*
Golding hops	*50 g/1¾ oz*
Hard water	*11 l/2½ gall*
Beer yeast	

Brew as for Light Ale (2).

Pale Ale

Pale malt	*1.125 kg/2½ lb*
Torrified barley	*56 g/2 oz*
Glucose chips	*225 g/8 oz*
Challenger hops	*42 g/1½ oz*
Hard water	*11 l/2½ gall*
Beer yeast	

Heat one gallon of water to 75°C/167°F, stir in the crushed pale malt and torrified barley, cover and mash to end point at 67°C/152°F. Sparge slowly with 4 pints of water at 75°C/167°F, then boil the wort and all but a good handful of hops for one hour. Leave for 15 minutes to cool, then strain into a bin, stir in the glucose, top up with cold water and, when cool, pitch an active yeast. Skim and stir on the second and third days, then add the rest of the hops, wetting them thoroughly. When fermentation is finished, rack, bottle prime, seal and store for two weeks.

India Pale Ale (1)

Pale malt	*1.35 kg/3 lb*
Crystal malt	*340 g/12 oz*
Flaked maize	*125 g/4½ oz*
Torrified barley	*125 g/4½ oz*
Golden syrup	*340 g/12 oz*
Challenger hops	*50 g/1¾ oz*
Hard water	*11 l/2½ gall*
Beer yeast	

Heat half the water to 75°C/167°F, stir in the crushed pale and crystal malts, the flaked maize and the torrified barley. Mash at 67°C/152°F until end point. Sparge slowly with half a gallon of water at 75°C/167°F, then boil the wort and all the hops for one hour. Leave to cool for 15 minutes, then strain out and press the hops, stir in the golden syrup and top up with cold water. Cover and leave to cool to 17°C/63°F.

Remove one pint of wort and store it in a sealed bottle in the refrigerator until required for priming. Pitch an activated yeast, skim and stir on the second and third days, then leave to ferment out. Rack into bottles, prime with the unfermented wort evenly distributed, seal and store for three weeks or longer.

India Pale Ale (2)

Pale malt	*1.125 kg/2½ lb*
Torrified barley	*250 g/9 oz*
Roasted barley	*125 g/4½ oz*
Wheat syrup	*125 g/4½ oz*
Flaked rice	*125 g/4½ oz*
Glucose chips	*450 g/1 lb*
Challenger hops	*35 g/1¼ oz*
Styrian hops	*15 g/½ oz*
Hard water	*11 l/2½ gall*
Beer yeast	

Heat one gallon of water to 75°C/167°F, stir in the crushed pale malt, torrified barley, flaked rice, wheat syrup and roasted barley. Mash at 67°C/152°F to end point. Sparge slowly with half a gallon of water at 75°C/167°F. Boil the wort with all the Challenger hops for 45 minutes, then add the Styrian hops and boil for a further 15 minutes. Cool for 15 minutes, then strain out, press the hops dry, stir in the glucose chips, top up with cold water and, when cool (18°C/65°F), pitch an active yeast. Ferment, skim, stir, rack, bottle, prime with caster sugar at the rate of half a teaspoonful per pint, seal and store for three weeks.

Bitter (1)

Pale malt	*1.125 kg/2½ lb*
Crystal malt	*250 g/9 oz*
Flaked maize	*125 g/4½ oz*
Golden syrup	*450 g/1 lb*
Challenger hops	*50 g/1¾ oz*
Hard water	*11 l/2½ gall*
Beer yeast	

Heat one gallon of hard water to 75°C/167°F, then stir in the crushed pale malt, crystal malt and flaked maize. Cover and maintain a temperature of 67°C/152°F to end point. Sparge slowly with 4 pints of water at 75°C/167°F, then boil the wort with all the hops for one hour. Leave to cool for half an hour then strain out and press the hops dry before discarding them. Stir in the golden syrup, top up with cold water and, when the temperature of the wort has fallen to 20°C/68°F, remove one pint of wort, seal and store in the refrigerator until required for priming. Stir in an activated yeast, then ferment to a finish, skimming and stirring on the second and third days. Rack into beer bottles containing an equal proportion of the unfermented wort, seal and store for at least two weeks.

Bitter (2)

Pale malt	*1.125 kg/2½ lb*
Crystal malt	*200 g/7 oz*
Flaked rice	*140 g/5 oz*
Weetabix	*14 g/½ oz*
White sugar	*450 g/1 lb*
Challenger hops	*35 g/1¼ oz*
Wye Target hops	*14 g/½ oz*
Hard water	*11 l/2½ gall*
Citric acid	*2.5 g/½ tsp*
Beer yeast	

Heat one gallon of hard water to 75°C/167°F, then stir in the crushed pale malt, the crystal malt, flaked rice and two crumbled Weetabix. Cover and mash at 67°C/153°F to end point. Slowly sparge with 4 pints of water at 75°C/167°F, add the acid, then boil the wort for 45 minutes with the Challenger hops. Add the Target hops, wetting them completely, continue the boil for a further 15 minutes, and then leave to cool for 30 minutes. Strain out, press dry and discard the hops, stir in the sugar and, when it is dissolved, top up with cold water. When the temperature has fallen to 20°C/68°F, pitch an activated yeast and ferment to a finish, skimming and stirring on the second and third days. Rack into bottles, priming each one at the rate of half a teaspoonful of caster sugar to the pint. Seal and store for at least two weeks.

Bitter (3)

Pale malt	*1.36 kg/3 lb*
Crystal malt	*200 g/7 oz*
Flaked barley	*200 g/7 oz*
Roasted barley	*70 g/2½ oz*
Glucose chips	*450 g/1 lb*
Hard water	*11 l/2½ gall*
Challenger hops	*35 g/1¼ oz*
Northdown hops	*14 g/½ oz*
Beer yeast	

Heat 10 pints of water to 75°C/167°F, stir in the crushed pale malt, the crystal malt, the flaked barley and the roasted barley. Cover and mash at 152°F to end point. Slowly sparge with 4 pints of water at 75°C/167°F, then boil the wort with all but a large handful of Challenger hops for 45 minutes. Add the Northdown hops and continue the boil for a further 15 minutes. Leave to cool for 20 minutes, then strain out, press dry and discard the hops. Stir in the glucose chips, top up with cold water and cool to 20°C/68°F. Remove one pint of wort and store it well sealed in a refrigerator until required. Pitch an activated yeast, skim and stir on the second and third days, then add the rest of the Challenger hops, wetting them thoroughly. At the end of fermentation, rack into bottles in which the reserved wort has been evenly distributed. Seal and store for at least two weeks.

Strong Ale

Pale malt	*1.35 kg/3 lb*
Crystal malt	*250 g/9 oz*
Roasted barley	*70 g/2½ oz*
Flaked rice	*125 g/4½ oz*
Brown sugar	*500 g/18 oz*
Northdown hops	*50 g/1¾ oz*
Medium water	*11 l/2½ gall*
Beer yeast	

Heat 10 pints of water to 70°C/158°F. (Add half a teaspoonful of salt to hard water.) Stir in the crushed pale malt, crystal malt, roasted barley and flaked rice. Cover and mash at 65°C/149°F to end point. Sparge slowly with 4 pints of water at 70°C/158°F, then boil the wort with all the hops for 45 minutes. Leave for 15 minutes, then strain out and press the hops. Stir in the brown sugar, top up with cold water, then cover and leave to cool.

Remove one pint of wort and store it well sealed in refrigerator until required for priming. Pitch an active yeast, then ferment, skim and stir on the second and third days. Rack into bottles in which the unfermented wort has been evenly distributed, seal and store for at least two weeks and preferably longer. This style of beer used to be called 'old ale'.

Brown Ale

Pale malt	*1 kg/2¼ lb*
Crystal malt	*250 g/9 oz*
Chocolate malt	*70 g/2½ oz*
Brown sugar	*250 g/9 oz*
Northdown hops	*35 g/1¼ oz*
Soft water	*11 l/2½ gall*
Beer yeast	
Lactose	*100 g/3½ oz*

Heat one gallon of water to 70°C/158°F. Stir in the crushed pale malt, crystal malt and chocolate malt. Cover and mash at 65°C/149°F until end point. Sparge slowly with 4 pints of water at 70°C/158°F, then boil the wort with all the hops for 45 minutes. Leave to cool for 15 minutes, then strain out

the hops, stir in the sugar and top up with cold water. When the temperature of the wort reaches 20°C/68°F, pitch an activated yeast.

Ferment under a cover and skim and stir on the second and third days. When fermentation is finished remove one pint of beer, dissolve in it the 3½ oz lactose and 1½ oz caster sugar for priming. Distribute this evenly between the bottles, then fill, seal and store them for two weeks.

NOTE: This is a traditional brown ale, not too alcoholic, nor hoppy, but with an off-dry finish. If a dry finish is preferred mash at 64°C/148°F and subsequently omit the lactose.

Stout (Dry)

Pale malt	*1.35 kg/3 lb*
Crystal malt	*250 g/9 oz*
Black malt	*125 g/4½ oz*
Roasted barley	*125 g/4½ oz*
Flaked rice	*125 g/4½ oz*
Weetabix	*15 g/½ oz*
Brown sugar	*250 g/9 oz*
Northdown hops	*50 g/1¾ oz*
Soft water	*11 l/2½ gall*
Stout yeast	

Heat 10 pints of water to 70°C/158°F, then stir in the crushed pale malt, crystal malt, black malt, flaked rice and two crumbled Weetabix biscuits. Cover and mash at 68°C/149°F to end point. Sparge slowly with 4 pints of water at 70°C/158°F. Add all the Northdown hops and, when they are thoroughly wetted, boil them for one hour. Leave to cool for 15 minutes, then strain out, press dry and discard the hops. Stir in the brown sugar and top up with cold water. When the temperature of the wort reaches 20°C/68°F remove one pint of wort and store it well sealed in a refrigerator until required for priming. Pitch an activated yeast and ferment at 17°C/63°F, skimming and stirring on the second and third days. Then leave to ferment out.

Rack into bottles in which the priming

wort has been evenly distributed, seal and store for two weeks at least.

NOTE: Before the yeast is added, check the specific gravity. The reading should be 1.040 or above. If it is not (because of inadequate extraction) stir in sufficient sugar to achieve this minimum reading.

Stout (Sweet)

Pale malt	1 kg/2¼ lb
Black malt	110 g/4 oz
Weetabix	15 g/½ oz
Brown sugar	200 g/7 oz
Northdown hops	35 g/1¼ oz
Soft water	11 l/2½ gall
Stout yeast	
Lactose	200 g/7 oz

Heat the water to 70°C/158°F and stir in the crushed pale malt, the black malt and the two crumbled Weetabix. Cover and mash at 64°C/148°F to end point. Sparge slowly with 4 pints water at 70°C/158°F. Add the hops to the wort and boil for one hour. Leave 15 minutes, then strain out the hops. Stir in the sugar and the lactose, then top up with cold water. When the beer is cool, pitch an active yeast. Ferment, skim, stir, rack into bottles and prime each one with caster sugar at the rate of one level teaspoonful per two pints. Seal and store for two weeks.

Barley Wine

Pale malt	2 kg/4½ lb
Crystal malt	500 g/18 oz
Roasted barley	85 g/3 oz
Brown sugar	750 g/1¾ lb
Challenger hops	50 g/1¾ oz
Hard water	11 l/2½ gall
Citric acid	5 g/1 tsp
Beer yeast	
Champagne wine yeast	

Heat 14 pints of water to 75°C/167°F and stir in the crushed pale malt, the crystal malt and roasted barley. Cover and mash at 67°C/152°F to end point. Sparge slowly with six pints of water at 75°C/167°F. Wet-in 1½ oz hops and boil for 45 minutes. Then add the remainder and continue the boil for another 15 minutes. Leave to cool for 30 minutes, then strain out, press and discard the hops. Stir in the sugar and citric acid and leave to cool. Top up with cold water and pitch an active beer yeast when the temperature reaches 18°C/64°F. Next day skim off the froth and rouse the beer thoroughly. Do this again on the third day. On the fourth day rouse up the beer again and pitch an activated champagne wine yeast. Leave the wort to ferment out, then move the bin to a cold place and add some finings.

After two days rack the beer into bottles and prime with 40 g/1½ oz of glucose powder dissolved in a little beer and distributed evenly between the bottles. Seal securely, store in a warm room for one week and in a cool store for one year. Serve in wine goblets.

Russian Stout

This is a very strong stout once popular with the Russian Court. Not widely available commercially but worth making at home if you like the taste of stout and enjoy a really strong beer. It is the stout version of barley wine. This recipe is for only 8 pints.

Pale malt	1 kg/2¼ lb
Flaked barley	125 g/4½ oz
Flaked maize	125 g/4½ oz
Brumore flour	125 g/4½ oz
Black malt	50 g/1¾ oz
Brown sugar	250 g/9 oz
Black treacle	20 ml
Northdown hops	20 g/¾ oz
Soft water	4.5 l/1 gall
Beer yeast	
Champagne wine yeast	

Heat 6 pints of water to 70°C/158°F and stir in the crushed pale malt, the flaked barley, flaked maize and black malt. Measure the Brumore flour into a basin and stir in enough cold water to make a smooth paste. Empty this into the mashing bin and stir well to ensure an even distribution. Cover and mash at 65°C/149°F to end point. Strain out the grains and sparge them slowly with three pints of water at 70°C/158°F. Wet-in the hops and boil them for one hour, at times without a lid so as to reduce the volume by one-eighth. Leave to cool for half an hour then strain out, press dry and discard the hops. Stir in the brown sugar and black treacle (20 ml = one rounded tablespoon), cover and leave to cool. Check the total quantity, which should be not more than $8\frac{1}{2}$ pints, and the specific gravity, which should be between 1.080 and 1.095, depending on your extraction rate.

Pitch an active beer yeast and ferment in the usual way, skimming and stirring on the second and third days. On the fourth day stir in an activated champagne wine yeast and, if possible, transfer the brew to a demijohn and fit an airlock. Ferment to a finish, then move the jar to a cold place to encourage the beer to clear. Siphon into beer bottles, prime with caster sugar at the rate of half a teaspoonful per pint, seal and store in a warm place for one week and in a cool place for one year. Serve in wine goblets.

Lager

Lager malt grains	$1.125\,kg/2\frac{1}{2}\,lb$
Flaked maize	$200\,g/7\,oz$
Glucose chips	$250\,g/9\,oz$
Hallertau hops	$35\,g/1\frac{1}{4}\,oz$
Soft water	$11\,l/2\frac{1}{2}\,gall$
Carlsberg yeast	

Heat one gallon of water to 60°C/140°F and stir in the crushed lager malt and flaked maize. Cover and mash at this temperature for one hour. Increase the heat to 70°C/158°F for half an hour, then cool to 60°C/140°F and maintain this until the end point is reached. Stir the mash to assist extraction after the first half hour, again when the temperature is to be raised, and again when the wort is to be cooled to 60°C/140°F.

Strain out the grains and sparge them slowly with 4 pints of water at 60°C/140°F. Add all but a handful of Hallertau hops and boil for 45 minutes. Leave to cool for half an hour, then strain out, press dry and discard the hops. Stir in the glucose chips, top up with cold soft water and, when the temperature has fallen to 20°C/68°F, pitch an activated Carlsberg yeast. Next day remove any froth or scum and transfer the bin to a cooler place where the atmospheric temperature is between 10° and 15°C/50° and 59°F. Leave the wort to ferment out, usually over a period of a few weeks. When fermentation has quite finished and the lager is clearing, siphon into bottles, prime with caster sugar at the rate of half a teaspoonful per pint, seal and store for three months.

This beer is slow to brew and mature. It is a waste of effort to try to hurry it. Serve it chilled.

Other beers

Never wholly satisfied with things as they are, mankind is ever searching for something better, or at least, different. This is as true of beer as it is of other matters.

If you think that you would like to try any of the following recipes, may I suggest that in the first brew you keep the quantity down to one gallon. This will give you a sufficient opportunity to sample the beer and will not be too much if you don't like it.

Long before the hop was universally adopted, various herbs were used, notably burdock, nettle and yarrow, and in Scotland the tips of spruce trees. You can buy botanical herbs and spruce essence from home brew or health food shops.

Nettle Beer

Malt extract	450 g/1 lb
Nettle tops	900 g/2 lb
Water	4.5 l/1 gall
Beer yeast	

The tops of young nettles can be picked, washed and boiled to flavour a malt wort. Collect only the top tender inches of young nettle plants, since the hard stalk is much too bitter to use. Wash them in clean, cold water, drain them fairly dry, then boil them in one gallon of water for a quarter of an hour in a covered pan. The nettles take up a lot of room, so a large pan is required. Strain the liquor into a bin and press the nettles with the back of a wooden or plastic spoon before discarding them. Stir in the malt, cover the

bin and leave to cool. Mix in an activated yeast and ferment out, skimming and stirring as necessary. Siphon into sterilized beer bottles, prime, seal and store for two weeks.

Spruce Beer

Instead of nettle tops, flavour the wort with two teaspoonsful (10 ml) of spruce extract.

Botanic Beer

Replace the nettle tops with a sachet of botanical herbs. The manufacturer will indicate on the packet how the herbs should be used, i.e., boiled with the malt, or steeped in hot water until it cools, or suspended in the fermenting beer.

Treacle Ale

Sometimes called black beer, in the past it was made by people living far from shops, who had few local ingredients.

Golden syrup	450 g/1 lb
Black treacle	225 g/½ lb
Water	4 l/7 pints
Beer yeast and nutrient	

Dissolve the syrup and treacle in one litre of warm water, add the remaining three litres cold, stir well and mix in the yeast. Cover and ferment to a finish. Siphon into beer bottles, prime, seal and store for one week. This is a thin, very dry beer with a strong flavour.

Honey Beer

Brown honey	*450 g/1 lb*
Hops	*15 g/½ oz*
Juice of 1 lemon	
Water to	*4.5 l/1 gall*
Beer yeast and nutrient	

Boil the hops in 4 pints of water for 30 minutes. Strain out the hops through a fine meshed nylon sieve, pressing them with the back of a plastic spoon. Stir in the honey and boil for a further 5 minutes, skimming off any scum that appears. Top up with cold water and, when the wort is cool, mix in the expressed and strained lemon juice and an activated yeast and nutrient. Cover, ferment, skim, rack, bottle, prime, seal and store for one week as described for other beers.

Ginger Beer

Root ginger	*28 g/1 oz*
Fresh lemon	*1*
Cream of tartar	*14 g/½ oz*
White sugar	*225 g/8 oz*
Water (hot)	*4.3 l/7½ pints*
Yeast	

Grate fresh ginger or well-hammered dried ginger and place it in a bin. Thinly pare the lemon, chop up the parings and add to the ginger. Pour the hot water into the bin and mix in the cream of tartar, the sugar and the expressed and strained juice of the lemon. Cover and leave to cool. Mix in an activated yeast and ferment in the bin for 24 hours. Skim off any scum that arises and stir well but gently. Replace the cover and continue fermentation.

Next day start checking the specific gravity with a hydrometer and, as soon as the reading reaches 1.002, siphon the beer into strong bottles, sweeten with two saccharins per pint, seal and store for four days. No priming is necessary, since there will be enough residual sugar to continue the fermentation and produce the effervescence. The saccharin will produce the necessary sweetening. Chill the beer before opening the bottles.

WARNING: Adding more sugar than recommended or bottling too soon could produce too much gas and possibly cause a bottle to burst. At best, the beer would erupt in foam when the bottle was opened.

Cock Ale

This is a very old recipe that was much loved by farmers. It has been adapted for home brewing.

Malt extract	*450 g/1 lb*
Hops	*28 g/1 oz*
Sugar	*225 g/8 oz*
Water	*4 l/7 pints*
White wine	*225 ml/½ pint*
Chicken pieces	
Beer yeast	

Boil the hops in 1 litre/1¾ pints of water for 15 minutes, then strain into a bin in which the malt extract and hops have been dissolved in 1 litre of warm water. Add another litre of water to the hops and boil them for a further 15 minutes. Strain this liquor into the bin, add another litre of water to the hops and boil this for the third time. Strain the now weak hop liquor into the bin, discard the hops, cover the bin and leave to cool.

Take the wing tips, tail, trimmings and bone carcase of a plainly roasted chicken that has just been served for a meal, chop up the pieces and place them in a basin. Pour on half a pint of dry white wine, cover and leave in a refrigerator until required.

When the wort is cool, add an activated yeast, cover and leave to ferment. Next day, remove any scum and stir well. Now strain the wine from the chicken into the wort and then suspend in it all the chicken pieces in a muslin bag. Replace the cover and leave for two days. Remove the bag of chicken pieces and discard them after squeezing out any flavoured beer. Replace the cover and leave for a further three days to finish fermenting. Rack into beer bottles, prime, seal and store for three weeks. Surprising though it may seem, this is a remarkably well-flavoured and enjoyable beer. Serve it cool in goblet glasses.

Cherry Ale

Many kinds of fruit may be used to add flavour to beer. If the flavour is very strong the fruit may be used instead of hops, but a better method is to make a lightly hopped ale and steep crushed fruit in it, rather like the recipe for cock ale. Another recipe is as follows:

Strong ale	2.25 l/4 pints
Morello cherries	450 g/1 lb
Demerara sugar	450 g/1 lb
Wine yeast	

Stalk and wash the black-ripe cherries, then open them and remove the stones. Place them in a suitable vessel, for example, a large sweet jar. Sprinkle on the sugar and stir so as to coat all the cherries with sugar. Cover and leave for 24 hours. Pour the strong ale on to the sugared cherries in such a manner as to cause the minimum of foam. Mix in a wine yeast, stir gently to dissolve the sugar, then cover and leave to ferment out. Siphon the cherry ale into sterilized bottles and serve in wine goblets. This beer is very strong and has a sweet finish with a delicious flavour.

Mulled Ale

Strong beers lend themselves to mulling better than light ales and lagers. In the days of open fires, an iron poker would be heated in the fire until the end was red hot. It would then be withdrawn, tapped on the hearth to knock off the ash, then plunged into a mug of strong ale. Sometimes a little ginger or some other spice would be added, depending on the palate of the consumer.

Another way is to warm the beer in a saucepan with the spices of your choice to a temperature of 60°C/140°F. This figure is important because, although the beer tastes hot, it still contains its alcohol. Above 65°C/149°F the alcohol boils away.

Go easy on the spices at first. One piece of well bruised root ginger in one pint of beer is usually enough. More can always be added, but an excessive quantity of spices can only be reduced by dilution with more beer. Mulled ale is particularly good on a cold night.

Hints on serving

When fermentation is completed clarification can be assisted by moving the container to a cold place for two or three days. The colder atmosphere diminishes the thermal currents in the beer and the solid particles settle down. The fairly clear, sometimes bright, beer can now be bottled, primed, sealed and stored without throwing too much deposit.

All beers undergo a secondary fermentation from the priming sugar and throw a small deposit of dead and dying yeast cells. In most cases these settle very firmly on the bottom, especially in bottled beers. Cask beers are sometimes not quite so bright as bottled beers, although they should always be clear and free from haze.

Storing beer in a cool place or cooling it in the refrigerator just prior to serving helps to retard the release of the carbon dioxide. This makes it possible to pour a fully fermented, properly primed and conditioned beer from a bottle without lifting or disturbing the sediment, almost until it has all been poured. Handle the bottle carefully, remove the crown cap and slowly pour the beer down the inside of a jug, rather than into the bottom. The slow pouring prevents air entering the bottle in the form of large bubbles that would disturb the sediment. It is better

for the air to enter the bottle over the top of the beer as it is poured rather than through it. Keep the bottle at an even angle and, as the sediment slowly reaches up to the mouth, revert the bottle to the upright. With care, almost no beer is wasted.

The beer may now be poured from the jug into any size of glass or mug. Some people think that a mug made from glazed earthenware, pewter or even silver, keeps the beer cool and is therefore preferable as a container. However, these materials have the disadvantage of preventing the appreciation of clarity, colour and condition. It is a joy in itself to see the steady rise of the bead of bubbles to the creamy, foaming head. After a few mouthfuls of the beer, it should be possible to enjoy the froth of bubbles clinging to the side of the glass, poetically described as 'brewer's lace'. It is also a sign of a well-made and well-conditioned beer – another visible satisfaction.

Technically, the most suitably shaped glass is one attached to a foot by a short stem and curving upwards and inwards. It should also be of clear, colourless glass, free from embellishment of any kind so as not to distract or spoil the vision of the beer. The incurved top is an aid to head development and retention, since it concentrates the bubbles into a smaller area. Equally important, it concentrates the bouquet of fermented malt and the aroma of tangy hops as a feast for the nose. It should be clean and appealing, free from any trace of unpleasant odour resulting from poor ingredients, lack of hygiene, or careless brewing. For the best effect, then, do not overfill the glass, but rather leave a little room for the nose.

Glasses, indeed all beer-drinking containers, should be washed in a warm, slightly detergent water and then thoroughly rinsed with fresh cold water. Traces of detergent or grease in a glass diminish the head retention and condition of a beer, causing it to become flat. After rinsing, drain and dry the glasses or other containers and store them, mouth up, so that stale air does not get trapped in them. Before use, give them a polish inside and out with a clean, dry cloth free from lint.

Take equal care of the bottles, too. After emptying them, wash out the sediment, rinse with cold water and drain dry before returning them to the store. Before use, they must, of course, be sterilized.

Australians, Americans and Europeans prefer to drink their beer at a much lower temperature than do most people in Britain. Their beer is much lighter than British beer, being lager in style and containing less body or fullness and a less pronounced hop flavour. Home-brewed light ales and lager style beers may be chilled for a while and served at 9° or 10°C/48° or 50°F. Bitter beers, export or strong ales, brown ales, stouts and barley wines, however, are best poured and served at around 13° to 15°C/55° to 59°F. At room temperature all beers tend to gush and foam too much. They become difficult to pour clearly and cannot easily be drunk because of the large gassy head – although this soon subsides and leaves the beer rather flat. Temperature is important in serving beers and it is worth experimenting with your own brews until you find the level at which the beer pours well and tastes good. It can vary from brew to brew.

Beer should be enjoyable when drunk by itself – fresh, tangy, refreshing and satisfying. But it also makes a splendid accompaniment to many foods, especially cold foods. The salads that overwhelm most wines come into their own with beer – spring onions, radishes, celery, tomatoes and cucumber in particular. Similarly, with cheeses, the strong-flavoured cheddars accompany beer better than any wine, whether served whole or melted on toast. Cold meats, notably cold roast beef and jacket potatoes with butter, make a splendid accompaniment to a full-bodied, home-brewed beer. Pickles and sauces, too, which are anathema to wine, make good friends with beer. Serve beer with open sandwiches, fish and chips, or beef-burgers and, if more substantial food is not required, enjoy a potato crisp with your beer.

In short, don't just swallow your home-brewed beer as you would at a pub, but rather serve it at the right temperature in suitable glasses with appropriate food. Make the most of your beer – you made it.

Occasional problems

Lack of head and life

Fortunately, home-brewed beer doesn't suffer from many ailments. The most common, however, is lack of head retention and life, especially in beers that have had a low original gravity. There are several possible causes:

1   Beer needs time to develop condition during maturation. If it is served too soon after bottling, the priming sugar may not be fully fermented. Five or six days are the minimum; two or three weeks are better. For stronger beers two or three months are better still.

2   Insufficient priming sugar will obviously also cause lack of life.

3   Care should also be taken to ensure that the bottle seal is gas-tight. The merest imperfection in the seal could cause a slow leak of the gas and leave the beer in poor condition.

4   Poor quality ingredients, especially the use of stale or slack malt grains, can also be the cause of poor head retention. It really is a waste of time and money to use less than best-quality ingredients.

5   Grain-mashed beers from which an inadequate extraction has been obtained may also be a cause. It is very important to get the temperatures right, to mash with the right amount of suitable water until end point and then to sparge slowly with sufficient water at the right temperature.

6   Traces of detergent or grease can kill a head. Even touching the beer with buttery or greasy lips can suddenly diminish the head.

7   In addition to correct brewing from good ingredients with proper priming, sealing and maturing, head retention can be improved by the use of heading agents, obtainable from home-brew shops and used in accordance with the manufacturer's recommendation.

Poor flavour

This is almost certainly caused by poor ingredients, including the water used. Water is, in fact, quite often the cause. If you have any doubt about your tap water, then boil all the water in an open pan *before* you use it.

Imperfect hygiene is another cause of unattractive odours and flavours. Every surface that comes into contact with the brew or beer at any time must be clean and sterile. It is a waste of time and money to cut corners in matters of hygiene. After any piece of equipment, especially a bottle, has been in use for some time it needs an extra cleaning. Soak it in Chempro or bleach for 24 hours; then rinse it clean with plenty of cold water.

Vinegar taint

The sharp, sour taste of vinegar may develop if the beer is left uncovered or unprotected for any length of time. The vinegar bacteria are always present, often carried about by the tiny fruit flies that seem to appear from nowhere. If such a smell and taste develop there are only two options:

1   Discard the brew and thoroughly sterilize the container.

2   Convert the brew to vinegar. To do this,

add commercial vinegar to increase the volume of the beer by one-sixth (i.e., add one pint of vinegar to five pints of beer). Leave the mixture in a well-aerated container in a warm place for three months; then bottle, pasteurize in boiling water, seal and store.

Unprotected beer can also be infected by a fungus which looks like a powdery surface on the beer. This can be removed by carefully inserting a plastic tube into the beer and leaving it for some hours until the disturbance has completely subsided. Very slowly pour some other beer into the tube until the surface rises and the powdery film floats off. Two crushed Campden tablets per gallon of beer should then be added to kill any remaining fungi and the vessel should be sealed. Several days later the beer must be re-primed and sealed again. But it is better to avoid the problem in the first place.

Haze

A number of factors can cause haze in the finished beer. Grain-mashed beers can develop a starch haze if the mashing period has not been long enough to convert all the starch to maltose and dextrin. Check for it by adding a few drops of iodine to a tablespoonful of beer in a white saucer. If the beer darkens, then starch is present and some fungal amylase should be added in accordance with the manufacturer's instructions.

A protein haze is more difficult to identify. It is caused by too much nitrogen in the beer. Malt-extract beers rarely produce a protein haze but grain-mashed beers are susceptible. If you don't sparge the grains enough, maltose may be lost. If you sparge them too much, an excess of nitrogen will be washed out of the grain. The specific gravity of the mash should be checked and sparging finished just before the 1,000 reading is reached.

Protein should be precipitated by the tannin content of the hops during the boiling process – the hot break as it is called. If the boil is not sufficiently vigorous or long enough, this may not occur. The addition of carragheen moss during the boiling helps to precipitate the protein and is further assisted by rapid cooling. Moving the pan to a sink and running cold water over the lid is quite effective. Straining out the hops and topping up the wort with cold water also lowers the temperature rapidly and assists in the precipitation of the protein.

If a beer is stored in too cold a place or chilled too much before serving, a haze may develop but this will disappear as the beer warms up. Flocculent yeast can occur at any time but is not very frequently found. Usually a good beer yeast will ferment well and settle out firmly. Now and again a poor yeast will not settle and the beer must be fined with gelatin or isinglass in accordance with the manufacturer's instructions. Most home-brew centres sell beer finings, but indiscriminate use is not recommended.

Sluggish fermentation

Once fermentation has started, it should be continued between 15° and 20°C/59° and 68°F, preferably nearer the lower end. But if the fermentation becomes sluggish give the beer a thorough rousing and move it to a warmer place. Too high a fermentation temperature, however, can cause a bitter taste.

It is important to use a good-quality yeast and a sealed sachet of dried beer yeast granules is recommended. Because of the manner in which they are prepared and sealed in the sachet, they are more likely to be in good condition when opened. Always activate them and make sure that you pitch a strong and active colony. Rousing the wort thoroughly at the pitching and after skimming helps enormously to ensure a good fermentation. A gentle stir is not sufficient. A strong, rolling rousing, bringing the wort from the bottom to the top, is needed.

The covering of the container can also be a cause of a sluggish ferment. If the lid fits too tightly, the fermenting gas may not be able to escape and will inhibit the fermentation. Lay the lid on loosely or cover the bin with a thick cloth so that the escape of the gas is not prevented. A good yeast, the right temperature and thorough rousing together ensure an effective fermentation.

Yeast bite

Reference has just been made to the bitter taste that can develop if fermentation is conducted at too high a temperature. The same bitter flavour can also develop if the dead yeast ring around the fermentation bin at the surface of the wort is not removed when skimming and stirring. If the finished beer is left too long on its sediment a bitter taste will be imparted. Similarly, if too much sediment is carried over at the bottling stage, a bitter taste will develop. Prevention is simple but, once developed, the bitter flavour cannot be eradicated.

Bacterial infections

If hygiene has been skimped or omitted altogether, or if the beer has been left uncovered, it can become infected by spoilage fungi or bacteria. The beer develops a slimy, oily appearance. Although sulphite at the rate of 100 parts per million will kill off the infecting organisms, the flavour is likely to be poor and the beer should be flushed away. The container should receive a very special cleaning and sterilizing with Chempro. Happily, infections of this kind occur only rarely. Keep containers clean and covered and your beer will never be infected.

Specific Gravity Table

Specific Gravity 15°C/59°F	Sucrose in 4.5 litres/1 gallon		Probable % alcohol after fermentation to dryness
	grams	ounces	
1.006	90	3.2	0.4
1.010	138	4.9	1.0
1.014	183	6.5	1.6
1.020	252	9.0	2.4
1.026	320	11.5	3.2
1.030	371	13.2	3.7
1.034	418	14.9	4.3
1.040	494	17.5	5.1
1.046	555	19.8	5.0
1.050	603	21.3	6.5
1.056	678	24.1	7.3
1.060	726	25.8	7.9
1.064	766	27.3	8.5
1.070	841	30.0	9.3
1.076	910	32.4	10.1
1.080	963	34.2	10.6
1.086	1136	36.9	11.4
1.090	1081	38.5	12.0
1.094	1134	40.4	12.6
1.100	1198	42.7	13.4
1.104	1241	44.2	14.0
1.110	1319	47.0	14.9

The specific gravity reading before fermentation will be distorted by dextrins, resins, hop oils, minerals and organic debris. The real sugar content will be some points lower, depending on the style of the wort. After fermentation, alcohol will distort the residual gravity because it is thinner than water. Take the readings before and after fermentation, deduct the final gravity from the original gravity and the units of specific gravity fermented give the probable alcohol content. **For example:** A bitter beer with an original gravity of 1.046 and a final gravity of 1.006 has fermented 40 units. According to the tables a sugar solution with a specific gravity reading of 1.040 will produce approximately 5.1% alcohol.

Index